For Engineers & Designers

DraftSight Exercises

200 3D PRACTICE DRAWINGS

SACHIDANAND JHA

Dear Reader,

Thank you for choosing **DraftSight Exercises** book. This book is part of a family of premium-quality CADIN360 books, all of which are written by Outstanding author who combine practical experience with a gift for teaching.

CADIN360 was founded in 2016. More than 3 years later, we're still committed to producing consistently exceptional books. With each of our titles, we're working hard to set a new standard for the industry. From the paper we print on, to the authors we work with, our goal is to bring you the best books available.

I hope you see all that reflected in these pages. I'd be very interested to hear your comments and get your feedback on how we're doing. Feel free to let me know what you think about this or any other CADIN360 book by sending me an email at contactus@cadin360.com.

If you think you've found a technical error in this book, please visit
https://cadin360.com/contact-us/.
Customer feedback is critical to our efforts at CADIN360.

Best regards,

Sachidanand Jha
Founder & CEO, CADIN360

DraftSight Exercises

Published by
CADIN360
cadin360.com
Copyright © 2019 by CADIN360, All rights reserved.

Limit of Liability/Disclaimer of Warranty:

Examination Copies

Electronic Files

Disclaimer:

Preface

DraftSight Exercises

❖ This book contain 200 CAD practice exercises and drawings.

❖ This book does not provide step by step tutorial to design 3D models.

❖ S.I Unit is used.

❖ Predominantly used Third Angle Projection.

❖ This book is for **DraftSight** and Other Feature-Based Modeling Software such as Inventor, SolidWorks, NX, Solid Edge, AutoCAD, PTC Creo etc.

❖ It is intended to provide Drafters, Designers and Engineers with enough 3D CAD exercises for practice on **DraftSight**.

❖ It includes almost all types of exercises that are necessary to provide, clear, concise and systematic information required on industrial machine part drawings.

❖ Third Angle Projection is intentionally used to familiarize Drafters, Designers and Engineers in Third Angle Projection to meet the expectation of world wide Engineering drawing print.

❖ Clear and well drafted drawing help easy understanding of the design.

❖ This book is for Beginner, Intermediate and Advance CAD users.

❖ These exercises are from Basics to Advance level.

❖ Each exercises can be assigned and designed separately.

❖ No Exercise is a prerequisite for another. All dimensions are in mm.

❖ Note: Assume any missing dimensions.

EX-01

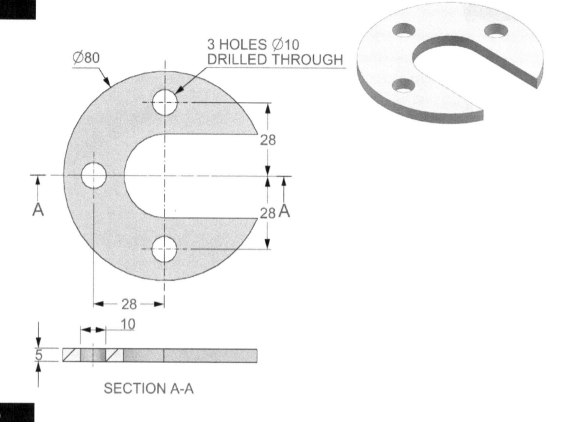

Ø80

3 HOLES Ø10
DRILLED THROUGH

28

A

28 A

28

10

5

SECTION A-A

EX-02

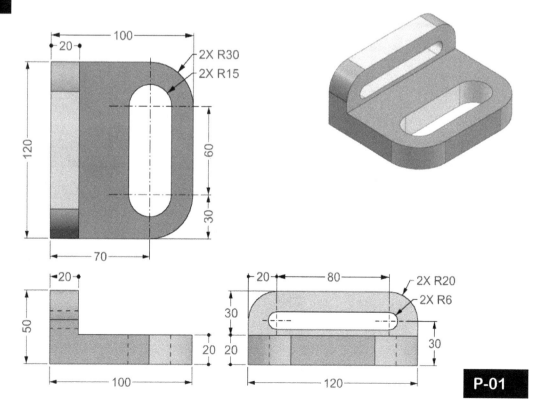

100

20

2X R30
2X R15

120

60

30

70

20

50

20 20

100

20 80

2X R20
2X R6

30

30

120

P-01

EX-03

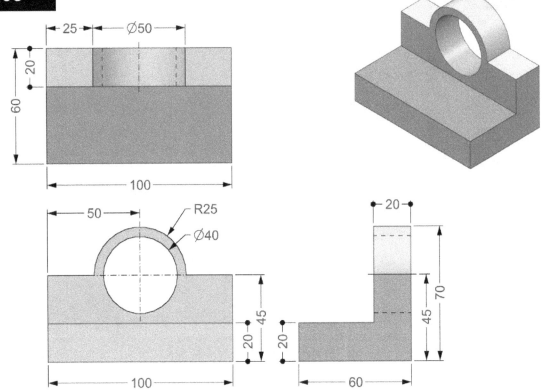

Top view dimensions: 25, Ø50, 20, 60, 100

Front view dimensions: 50, R25, Ø40, 45, 20, 20, 100

Side view dimensions: 20, 70, 45, 20, 60

EX-04

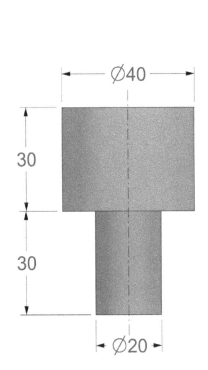

Ø40, 30, 30, Ø20

P-02

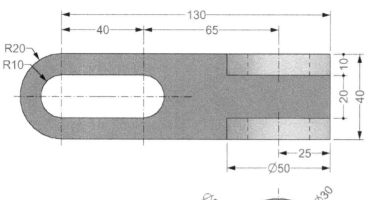

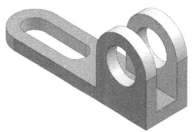

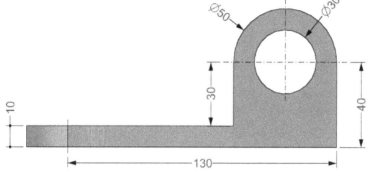

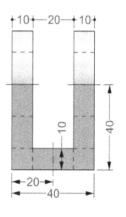

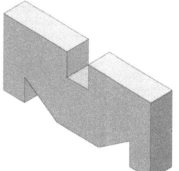

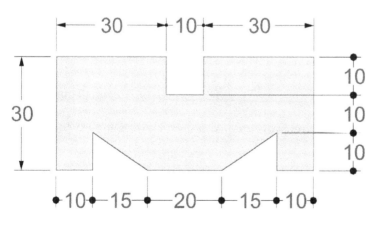

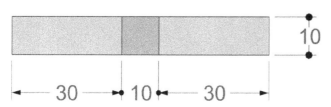

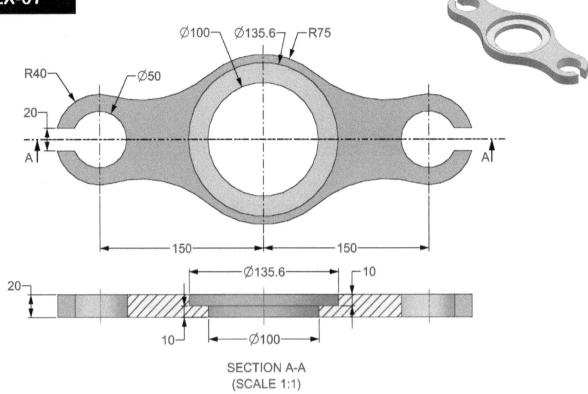

Ø100 Ø135.6 R75
R40 Ø50
20
A A
150 150

Ø135.6 10
20
10 Ø100

SECTION A-A
(SCALE 1:1)

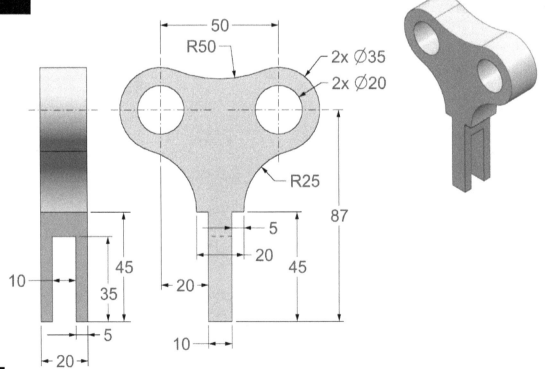

50
R50
2x Ø35
2x Ø20
R25
87
45
5
20
45
10
35
20
5
5
20
10
20

EX-09

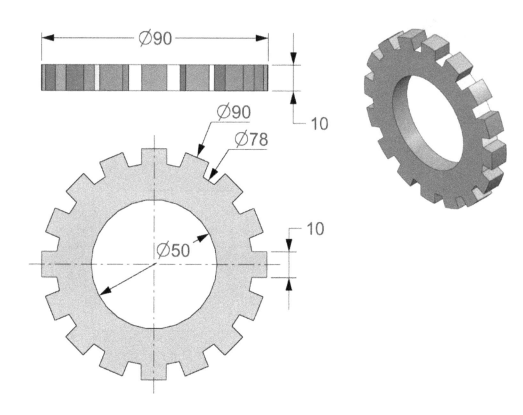

⌀90

10

⌀90
⌀78

10

⌀50

EX-10

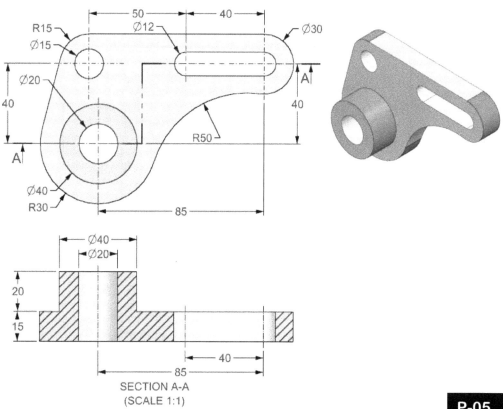

50 — 40

R15
⌀15
⌀12
⌀30

⌀20

40

40

R50

A

A

⌀40
R30

85

⌀40
⌀20

20

15

40

85

SECTION A-A
(SCALE 1:1)

EX-11

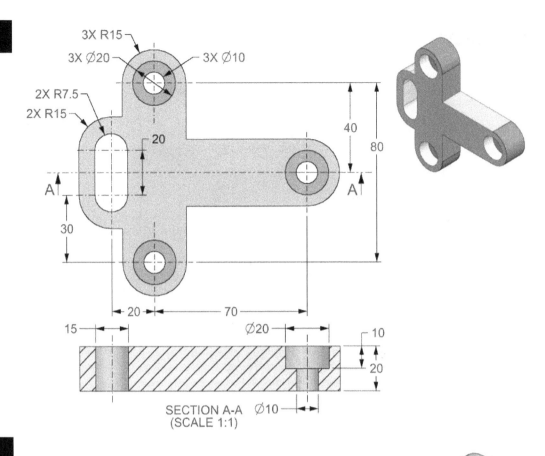

3X R15
3X Ø20
3X Ø10
2X R7.5
2X R15
20
40
80
A
A
30
20
70

15
Ø20
10
20
Ø10

SECTION A-A
(SCALE 1:1)

EX-12

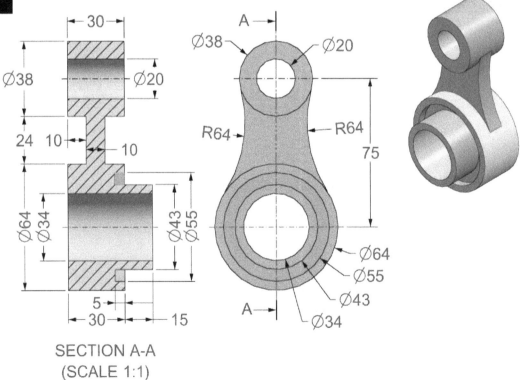

30
Ø38
Ø20
24
10
10
Ø64
Ø34
Ø43
Ø55
5
30
15

A
Ø38
Ø20
R64
R64
75
Ø64
Ø55
Ø43
Ø34
A

SECTION A-A
(SCALE 1:1)

P-06

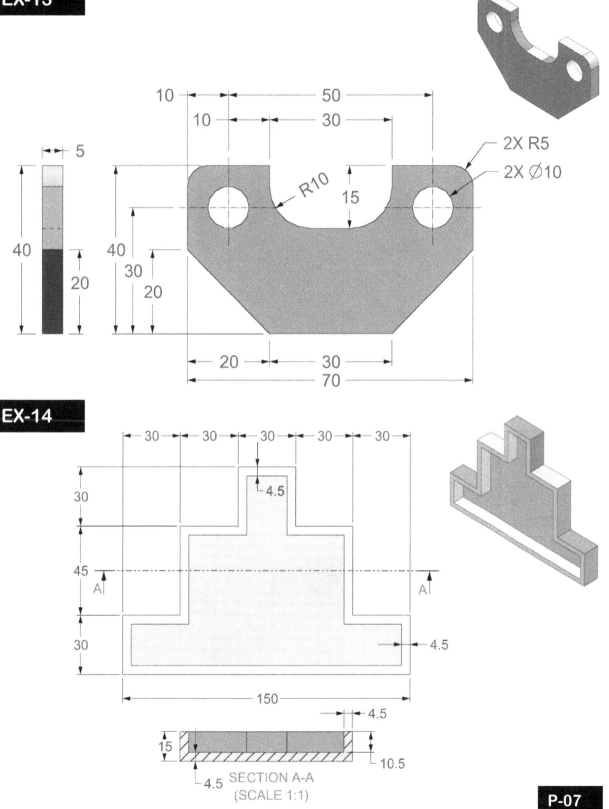

EX-13

10
50
10
30
2X R5
2X Ø10
R10
15
5
40
40
20
30
20
20
30
70

EX-14

30 30 30 30 30
30
4.5
45
A A
30
4.5
150

4.5
15
10.5
4.5

SECTION A-A
(SCALE 1:1)

P-07

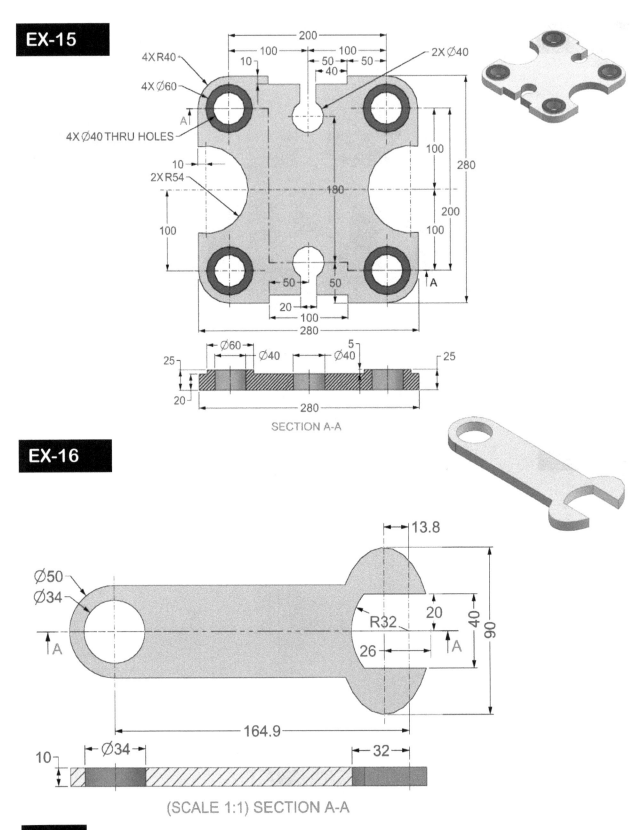

EX-15

4X R40
4X Ø60
4X Ø40 THRU HOLES
2X Ø40
2X R54

200
100
100
50
50
40
10
180
280
200
100
100
100
100
50
50
20
100
280

SECTION A-A

Ø60
Ø40
5
Ø40
25
25
20
280

EX-16

Ø50
Ø34
R32
13.8
20
40
90
26
A
A
164.9

Ø34
32
10

(SCALE 1:1) SECTION A-A

P-08

EX-17

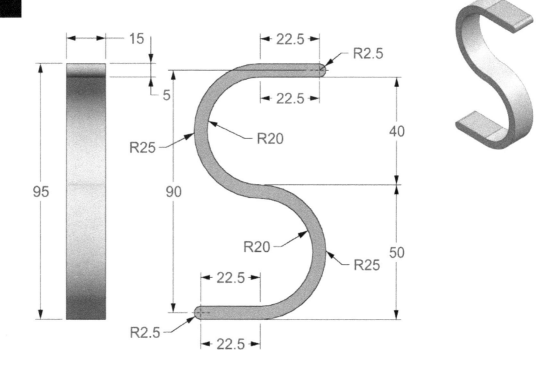

EX-18

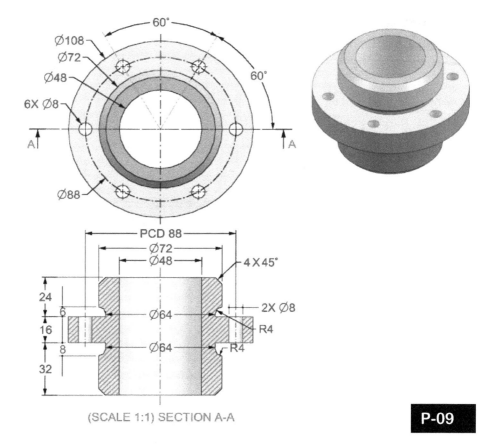

(SCALE 1:1) SECTION A-A

P-09

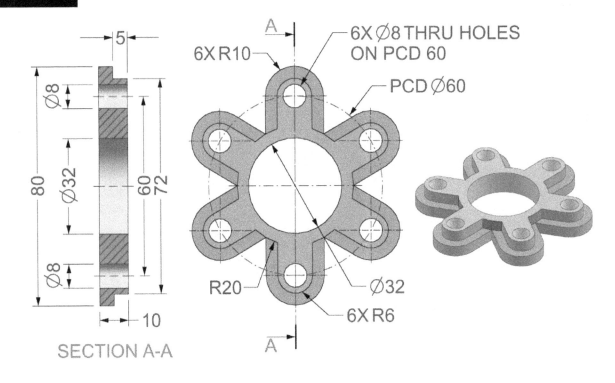

6X Ø8 THRU HOLES
ON PCD 60

6X R10

PCD Ø60

Ø8

Ø32

80

60
72

Ø8

R20

Ø32

6X R6

10

5

SECTION A-A

A

A

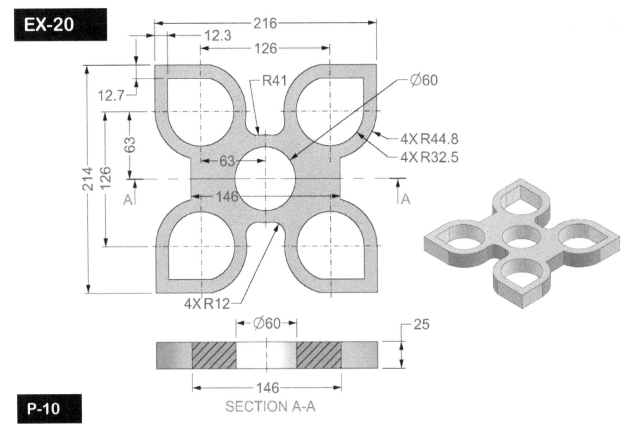

216

12.3

126

12.7

R41

Ø60

4X R44.8
4X R32.5

63

63

214

126

146

A

A

4X R12

Ø60

25

146

SECTION A-A

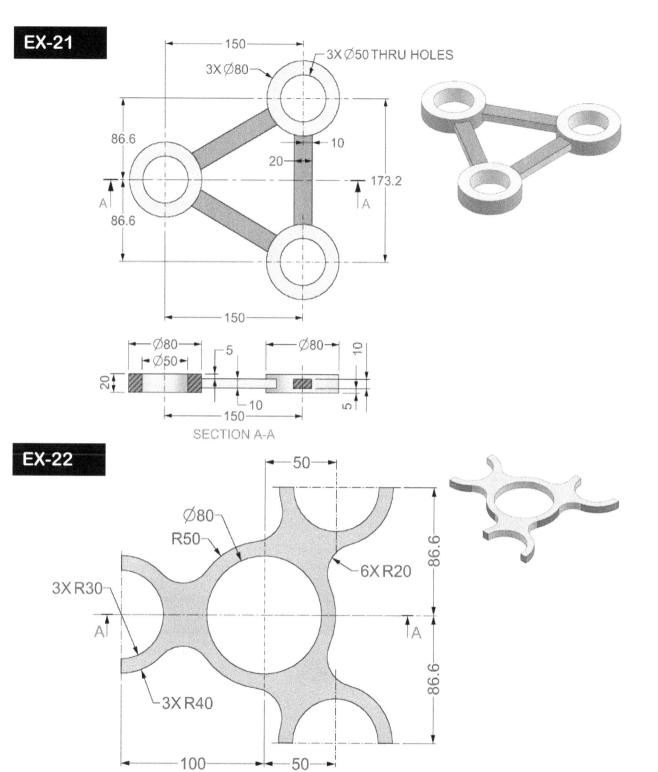

EX-21

150

3X Ø50 THRU HOLES

3X Ø80

86.6

10

20

173.2

A

A

86.6

150

Ø80

Ø50

5

Ø80

10

20

10

10

150

5

SECTION A-A

EX-22

50

Ø80

R50

86.6

6X R20

3X R30

A

A

3X R40

86.6

100

50

Ø80

10

Ø80

SECTION A-A

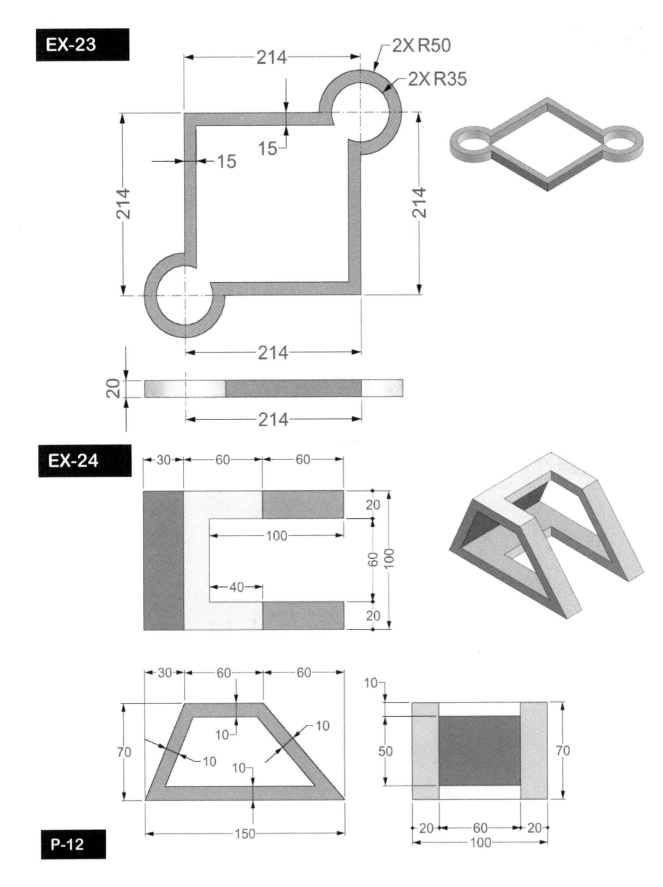

EX-23

214

2X R50

2X R35

15

15

214

214

214

20

214

EX-24

30 60 60

20

100

60 100

40

20

P-12

30 60 60

10

10

10

70

10

10

150

10

50

70

20 60 20

100

EX-25

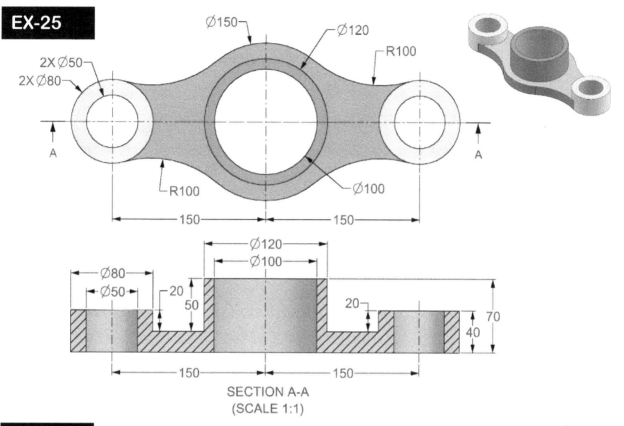

Ø150
Ø120
R100
2X Ø50
2X Ø80
R100
Ø100
150
150

SECTION A-A
(SCALE 1:1)

Ø80
Ø50
20
50
Ø120
Ø100
20
70
40
150
150

EX-26

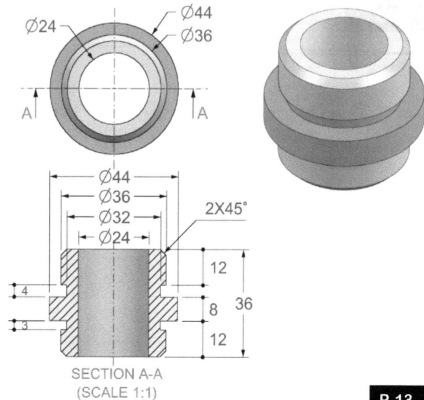

Ø24
Ø44
Ø36

A   A

Ø44
Ø36
Ø32
Ø24
2X45°
12
4
8
36
3
12

SECTION A-A
(SCALE 1:1)

EX-27

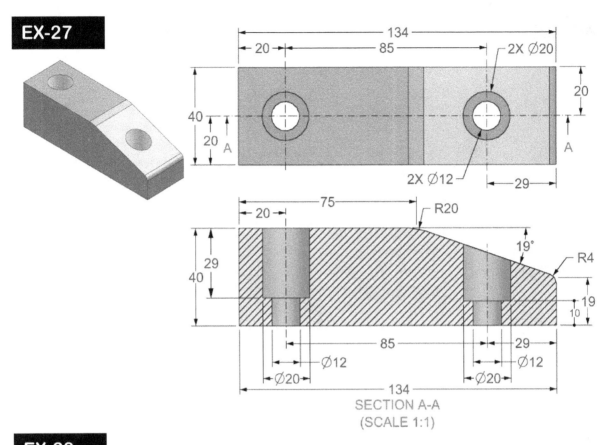

134
20
85
2X Ø20
40
20
20
A
A
2X Ø12
29

20
75
R20
19°
R4
29
40
19
10
85
29
Ø12
Ø12
Ø20
Ø20
134
SECTION A-A
(SCALE 1:1)

EX-28

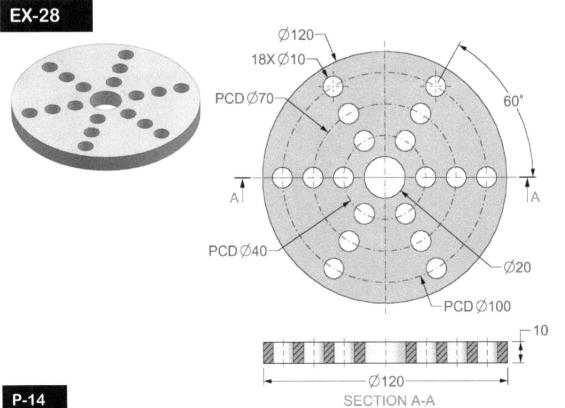

Ø120
18X Ø10
PCD Ø70
60°
PCD Ø40
Ø20
PCD Ø100

10
Ø120
SECTION A-A

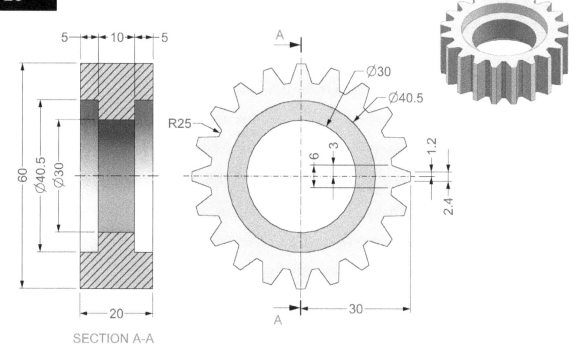

SECTION A-A

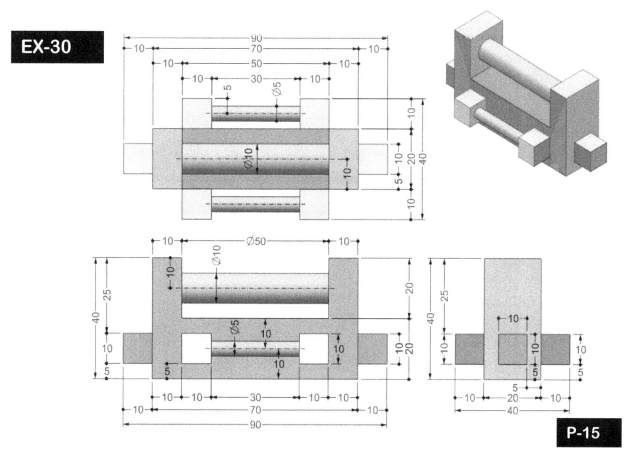

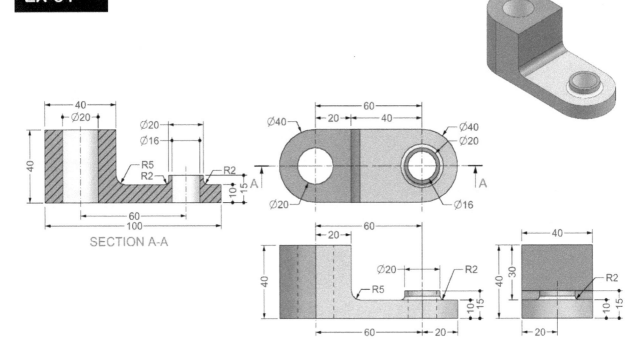

SECTION A-A

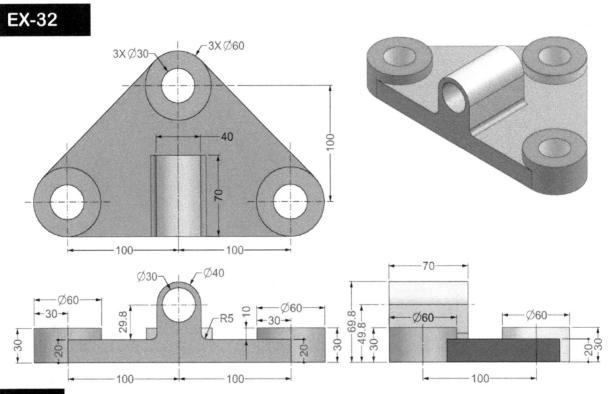

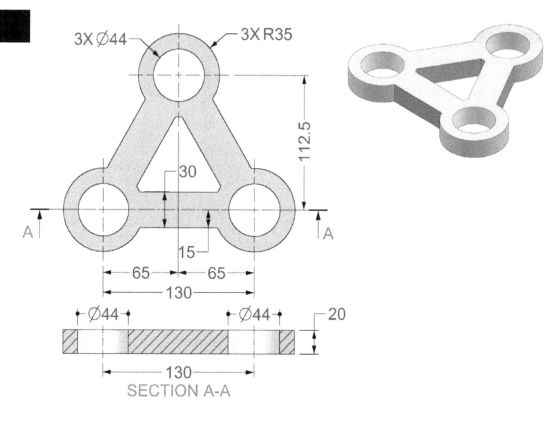

3X Ø44   3X R35

112.5

30

15

65   65

130

Ø44   Ø44   20

130

SECTION A-A

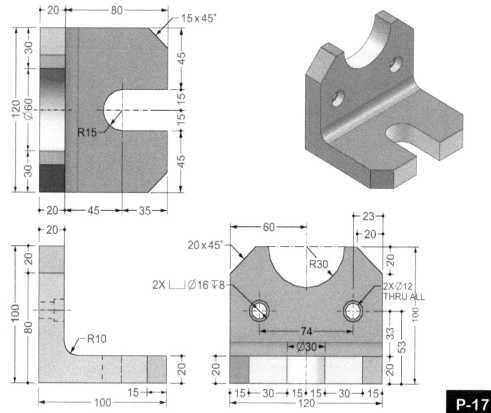

20   80   15 x 45°

30   45

120   Ø60   15 15

R15   15

30   45

20   45   35

20

20

100   80

R10

100   20

15

100

60   23

20 x 45°   20

R30

2X ⊔ Ø16 ↓8   2X Ø12 THRU ALL

20

74   33   100

Ø30   53

20

15 30 15 15 30 15   20

120

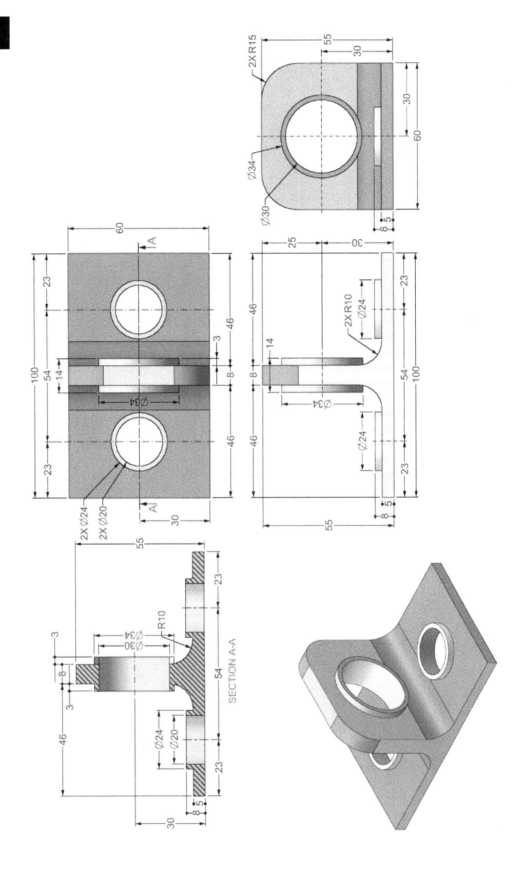

SECTION A-A

EX-36

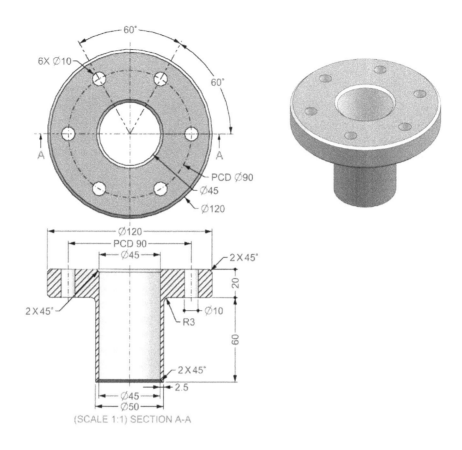

60°

6X Ø10

60°

A   A

PCD Ø90
Ø45
Ø120

Ø120
PCD 90
Ø45
2 X 45°
20
2 X 45°
Ø10
R3
60
2 X 45°
2.5
Ø45
Ø50

(SCALE 1:1) SECTION A-A

EX-37

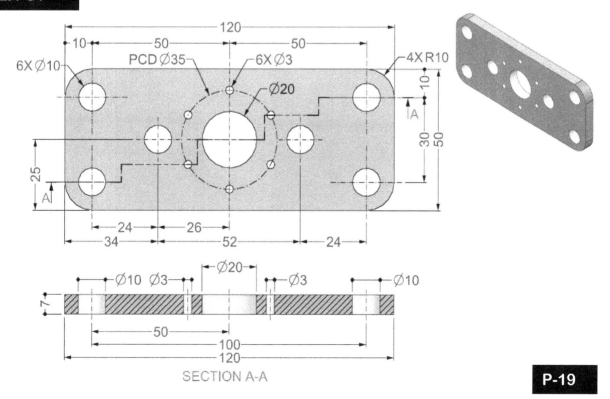

120
10   50   50
PCD Ø35   6X Ø3   4X R10
6X Ø10   10
Ø20
A
25   30   50
A
24   26
34   52   24

Ø10 Ø3   Ø20   Ø3   Ø10
7
50
100
120

SECTION A-A

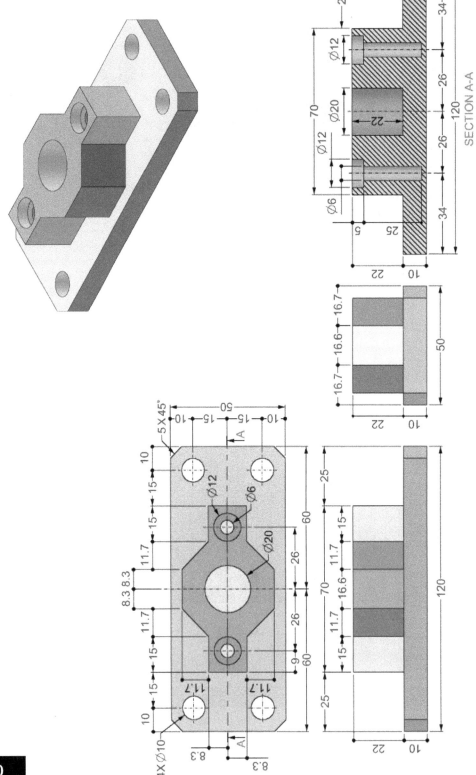

SECTION A-A

Ø12
Ø20
Ø12
Ø6
70
25
22
22
34
26
120
26
34
10
25
5

16.7
16.7
16.6
16.7
50
22
10

5X45°
50
10
15
15
10
A
Ø12
Ø6
Ø20
10
15
15
15
11.7
8.3 8.3
11.7
15
10
11.7
11.7
8.3
8.3
A
A
60
26
26
9
60
4X Ø10

25
15
11.7
16.6
11.7
15
25
70
120
22
10

EX-39

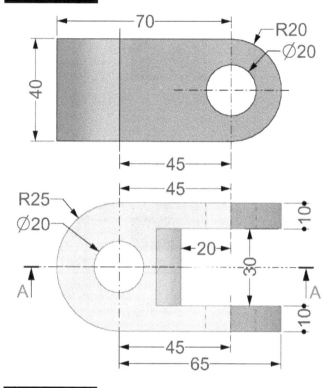

R20
Ø20
70
40
45

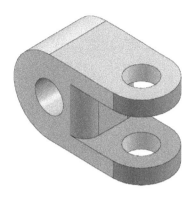

R25
Ø20
45
20
30
10
10
45
65
A
A

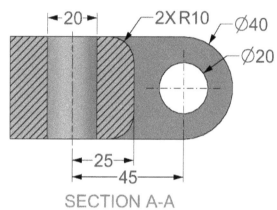

20
2X R10
Ø40
Ø20
25
45

SECTION A-A

EX-40

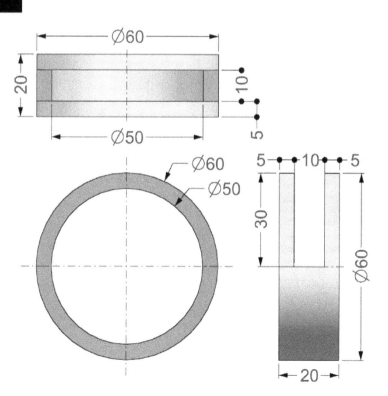

Ø60
20
10
5
Ø50

Ø60
Ø50

5
10
5
30
Ø60
20

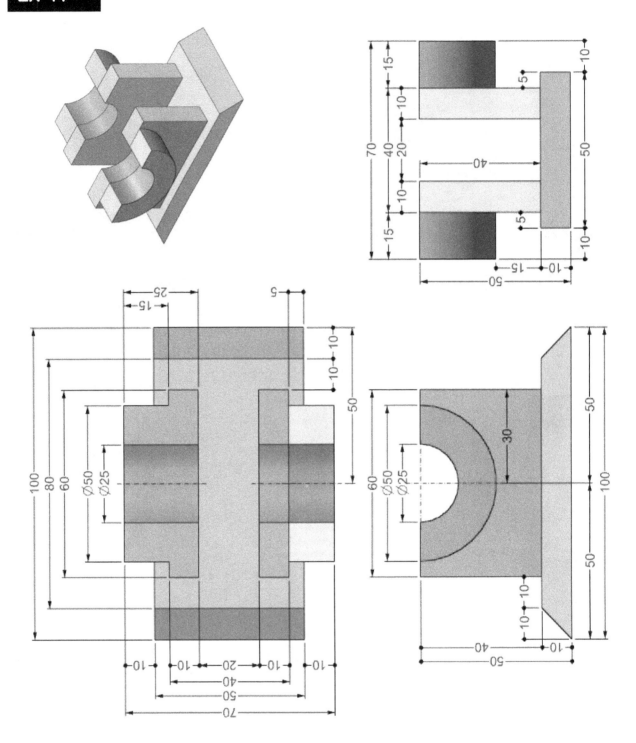

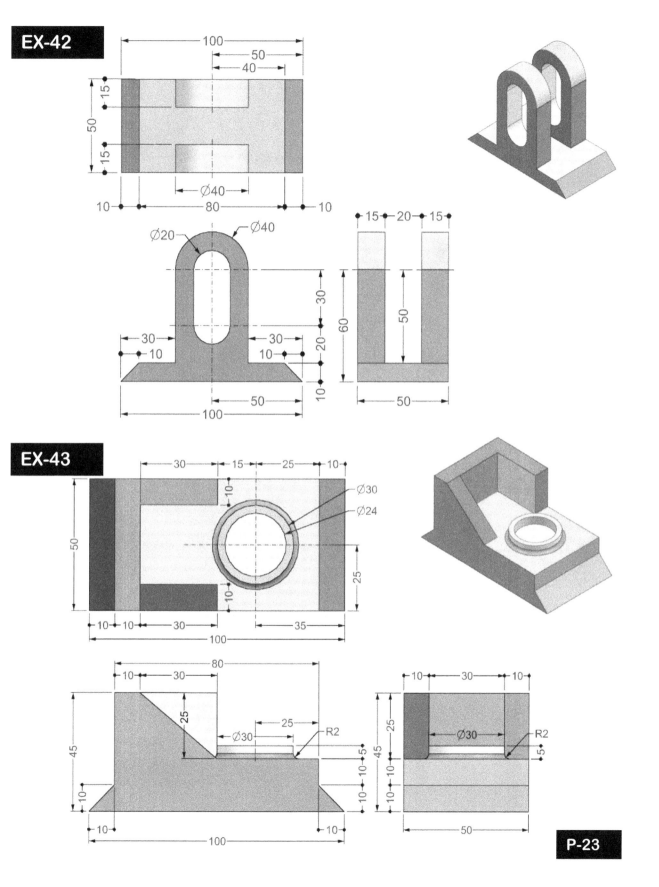

EX-42

100
50
40
15
50
15
Ø40
10   80   10
Ø20   Ø40
30
30   30
10   10   20
50   10
100

15   20   15
60   50
50

EX-43

30   15   25   10
10
Ø30
Ø24
50
25
10
10   10   30   35
100

80
10   30
25
Ø30   25   R2
45   5
10
10
10   10
100

10   30   10
25
Ø30   R2
45   5
10
10
50

P-23

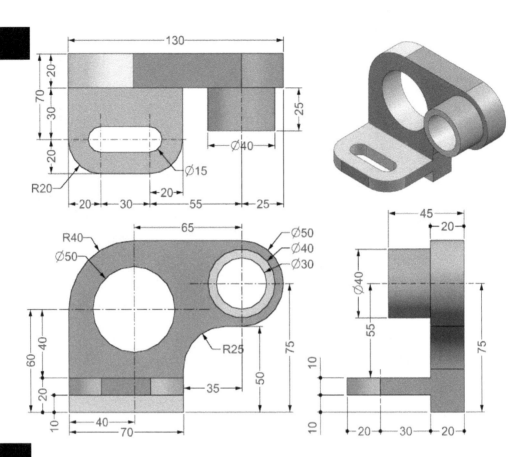

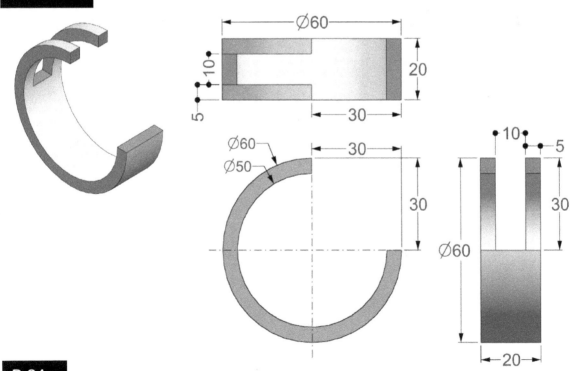

EX-46

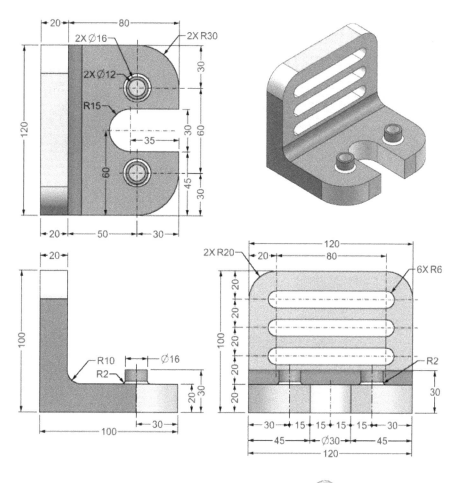

EX-47

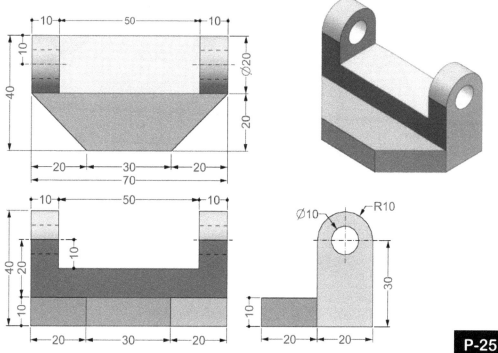

P-25

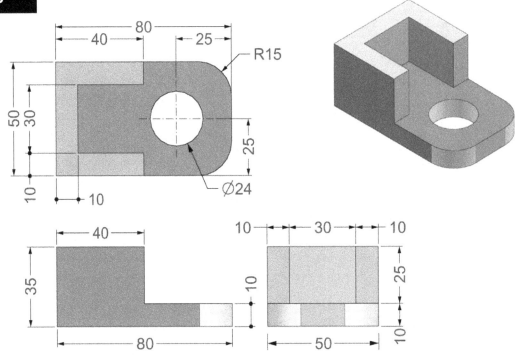

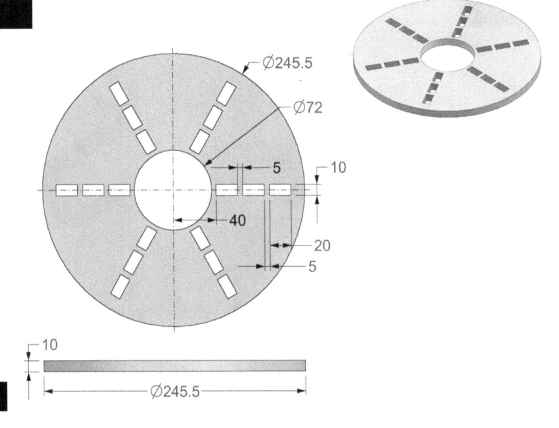

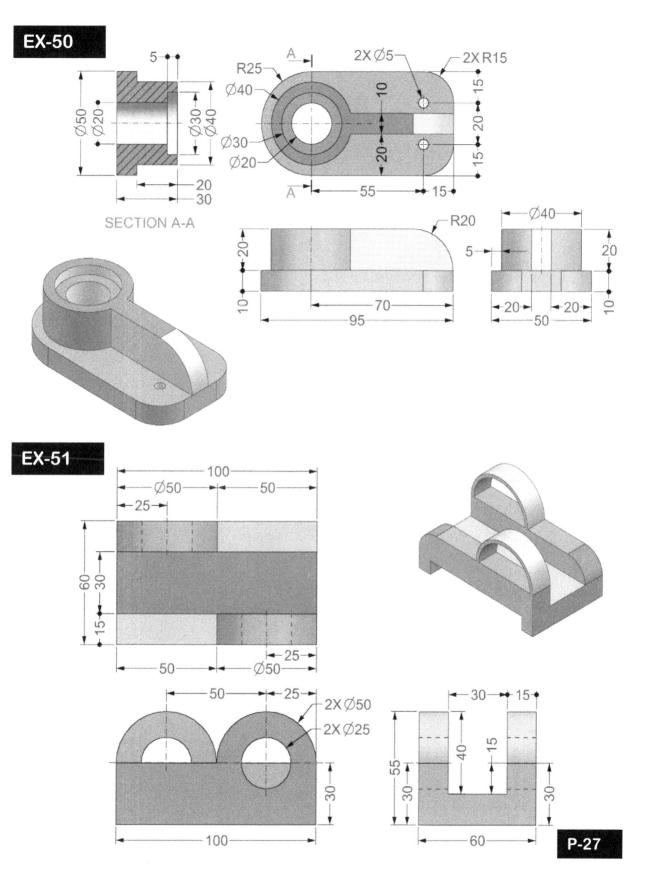

EX-50

SECTION A-A

2X Ø5
2X R15
R25
Ø40
Ø30
Ø20
Ø50
Ø20
Ø30
Ø40

R20
Ø40

EX-51

Ø50
2X Ø50
2X Ø25

P-27

EX-52

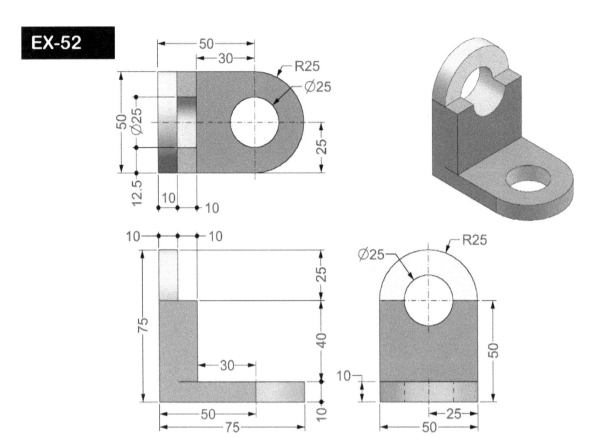

EX-53

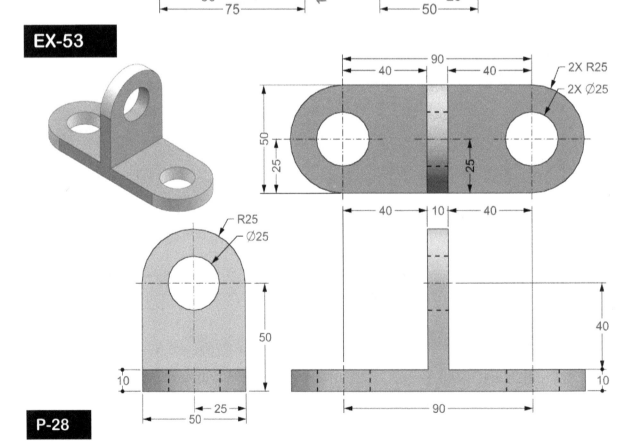

P-28

EX-54

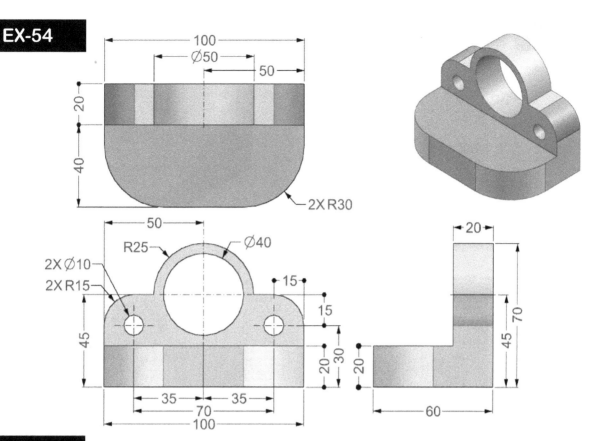

100
Ø50
50
20
40
2X R30

50
R25
Ø40
2X Ø10
2X R15
45
15
15
20
30
35
35
70
100

20
70
45
20
60

EX-55

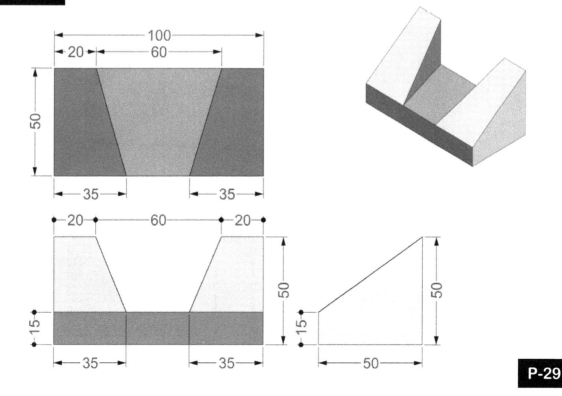

100
20
60
50
35
35

20
60
20
50
15
35
35

50
15
50

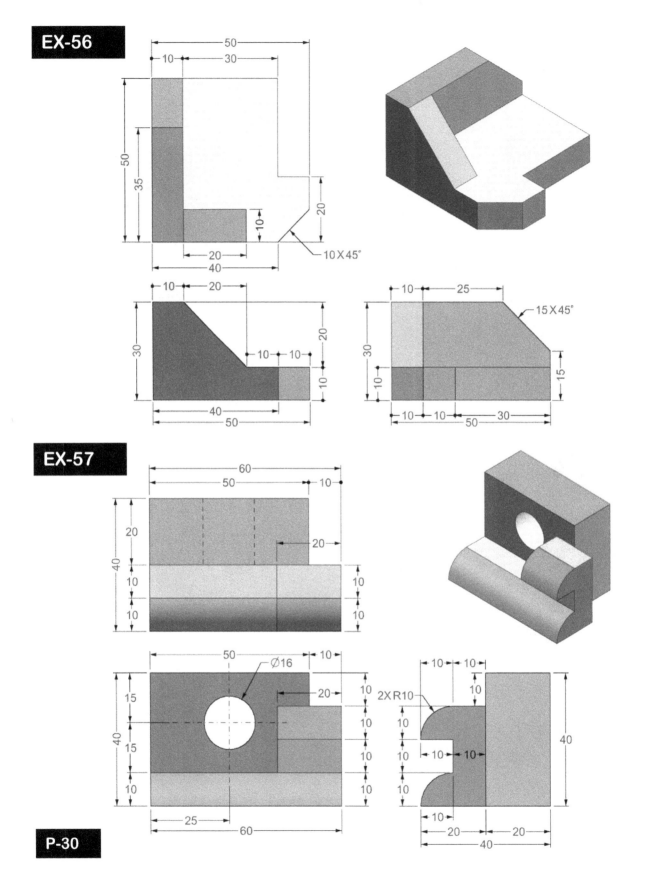

EX-56

EX-57

P-30

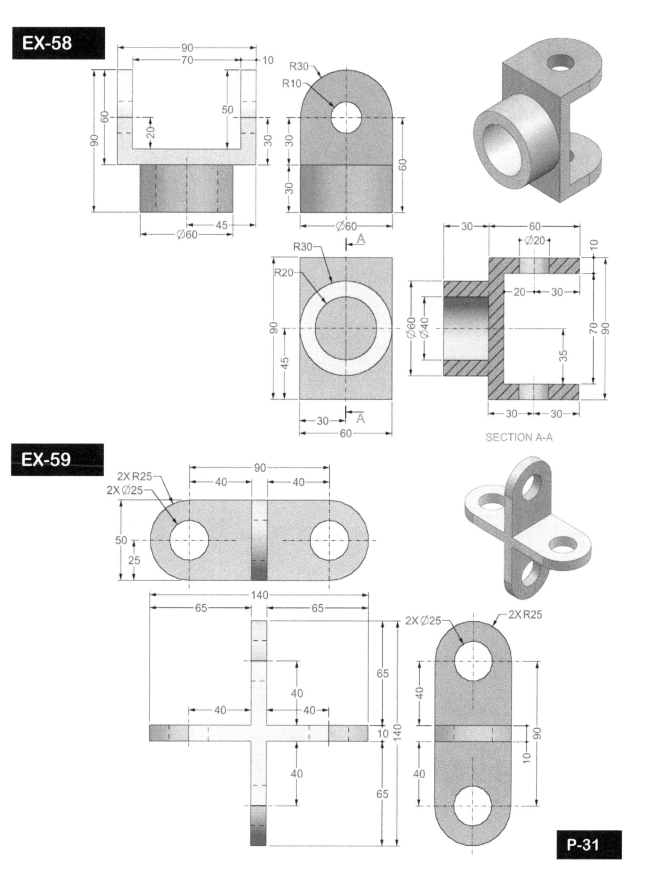

EX-58

R30
R10
R30
R20
SECTION A-A

EX-59

2X R25
2X Ø25
2X Ø25
2X R25

P-31

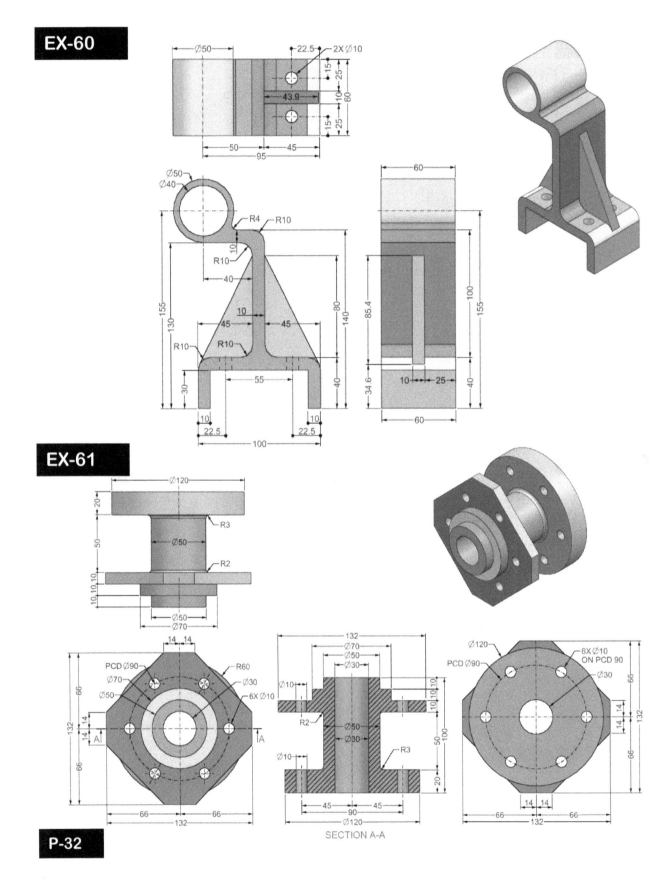

EX-60

EX-61

P-32

SECTION A-A

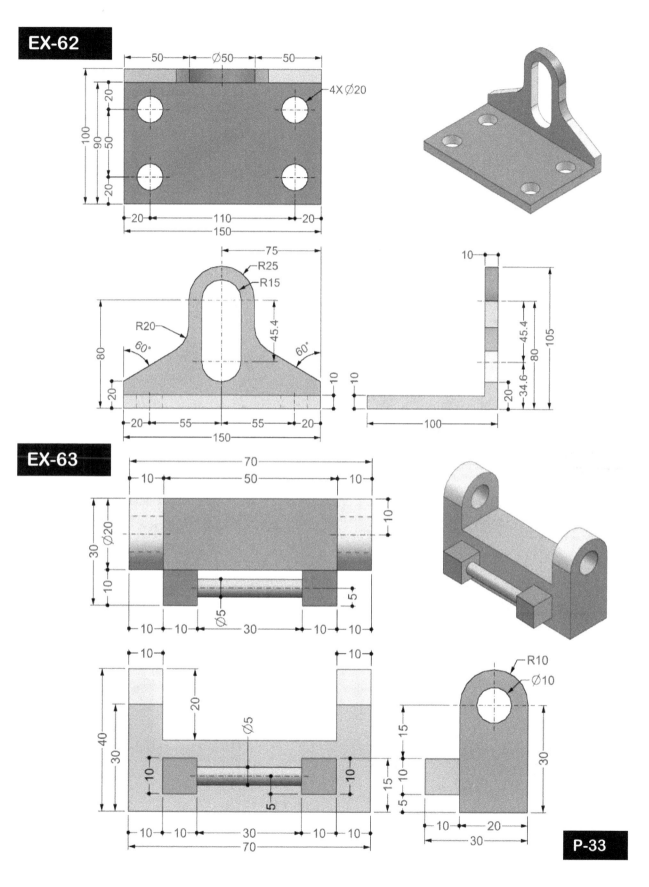

EX-62

EX-63

P-33

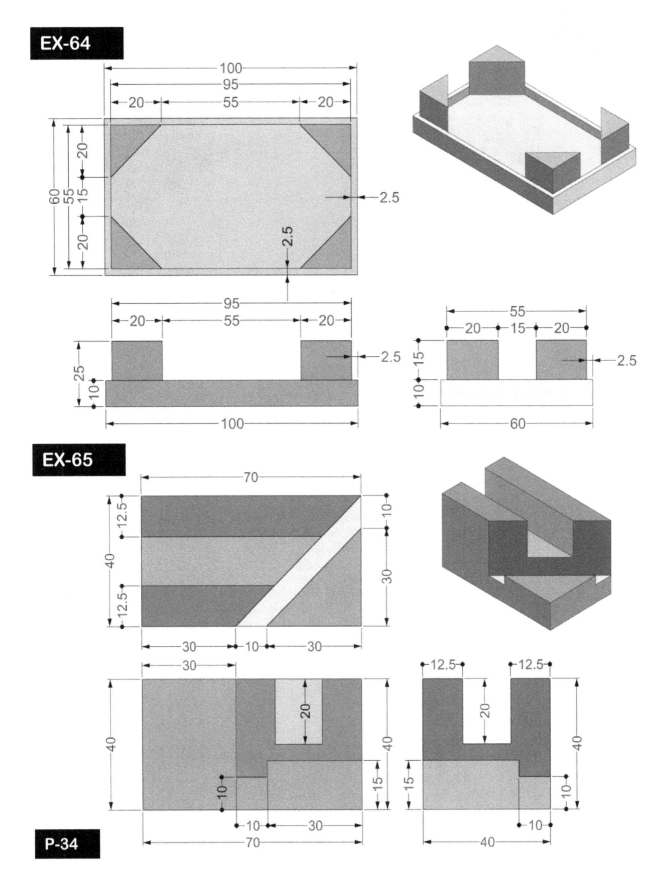

EX-64

EX-65

P-34

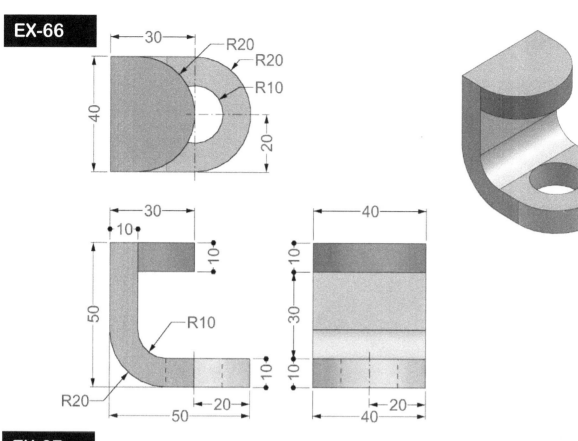

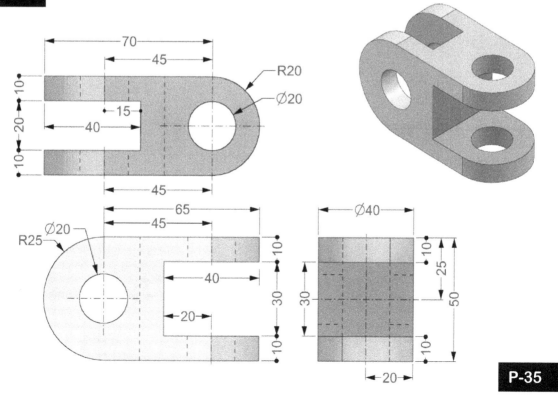

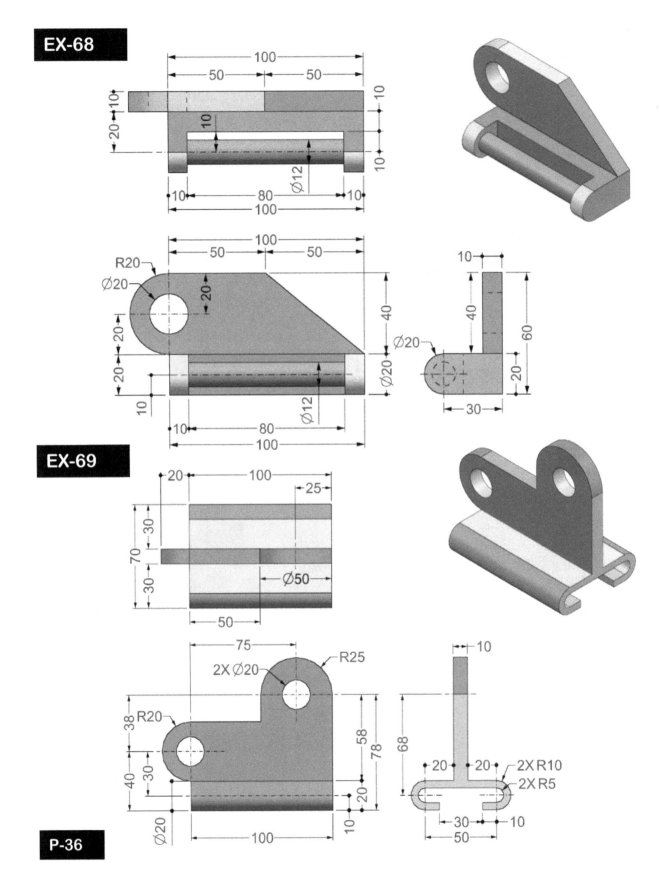

EX-68

EX-69

P-36

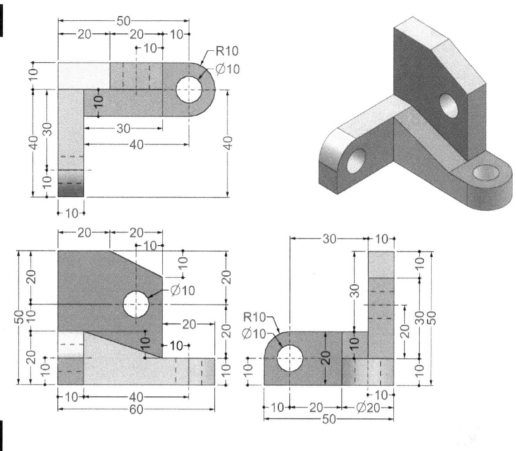

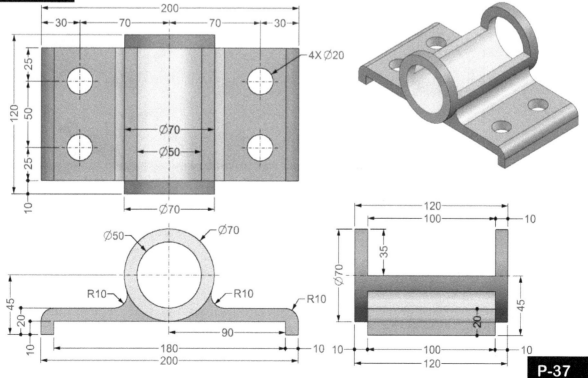

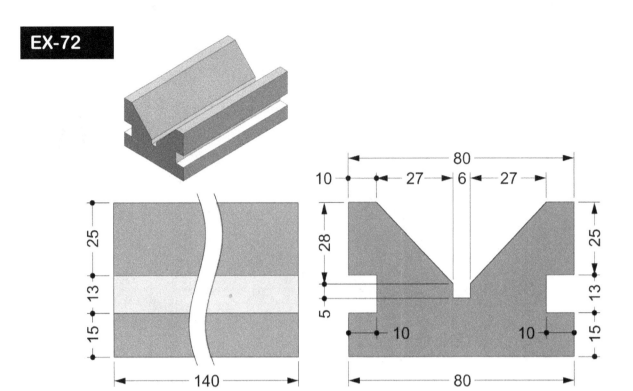

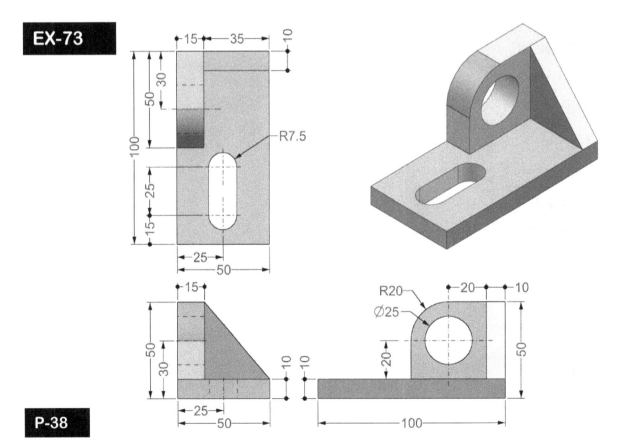

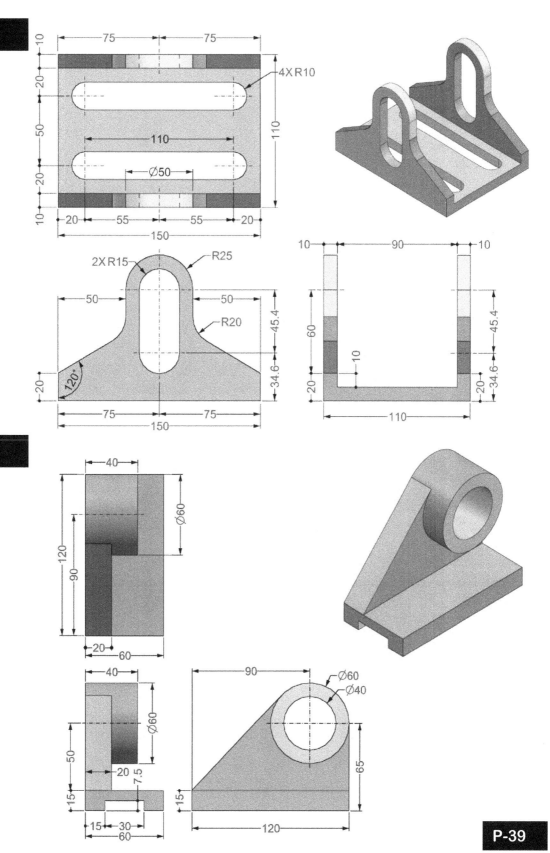

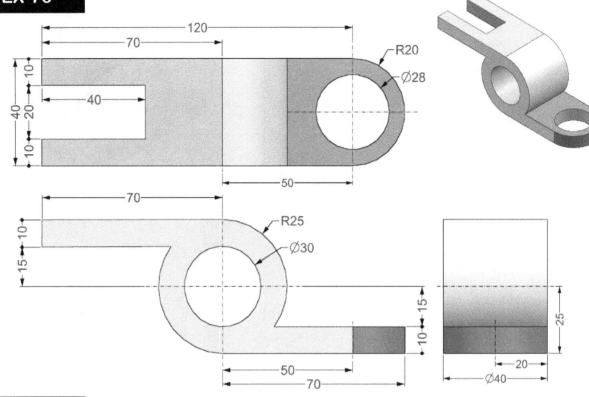

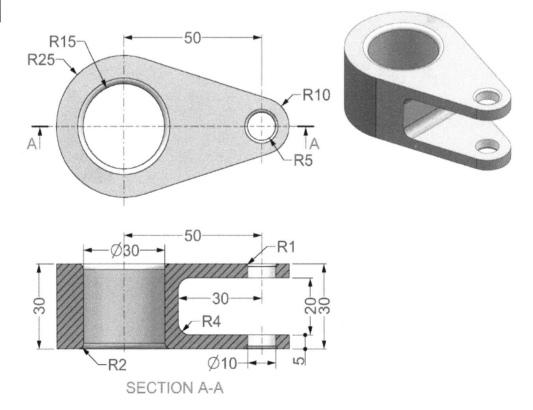

SECTION A-A

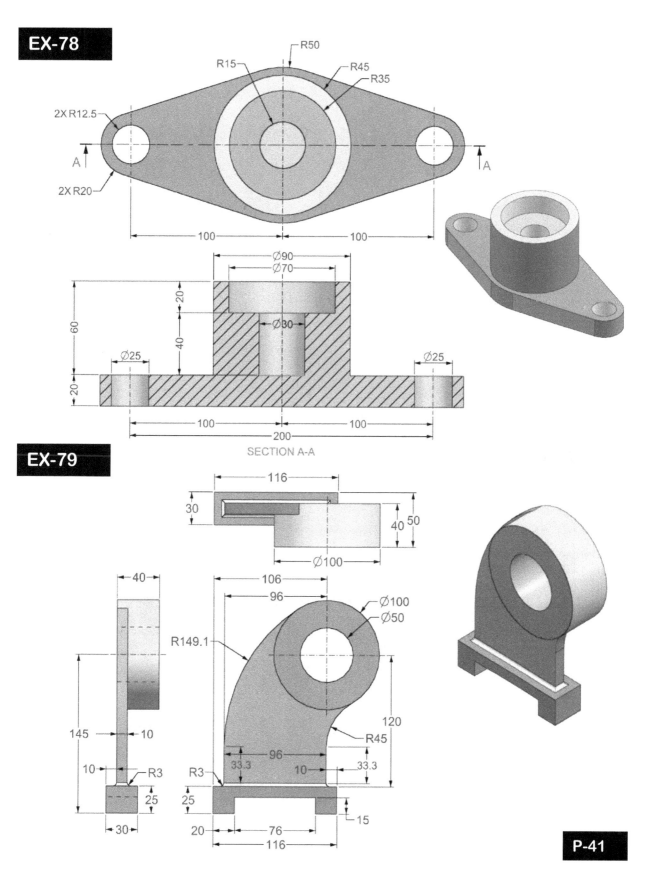

EX-78

R50
R15
R45
R35
2X R12.5
A
2X R20
100
100

Ø90
Ø70
20
60
40
Ø30
Ø25
Ø25
20
100
100
200

SECTION A-A

EX-79

116
30
40 50
Ø100

40
106
96
Ø100
Ø50
R149.1
120
145
10
R45
10
R3
96
33.3
10
33.3
25
R3
25
30
20
76
15
116

P-41

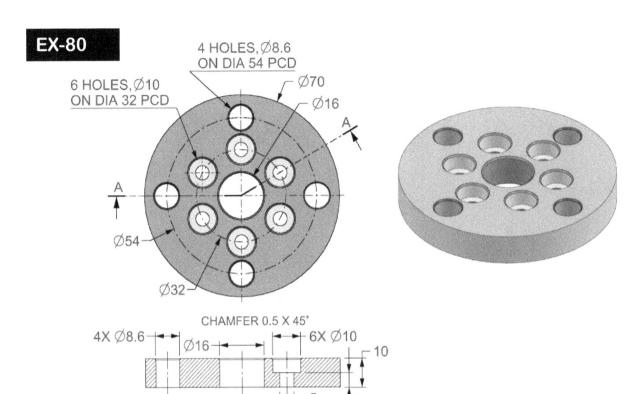

4 HOLES, ∅8.6
ON DIA 54 PCD

6 HOLES, ∅10
ON DIA 32 PCD

∅70

∅16

A

A

∅54

∅32

CHAMFER 0.5 X 45°

4X ∅8.6

∅16

6X ∅10

10

5

5

SECTION A-A
(SCALE 1:1)

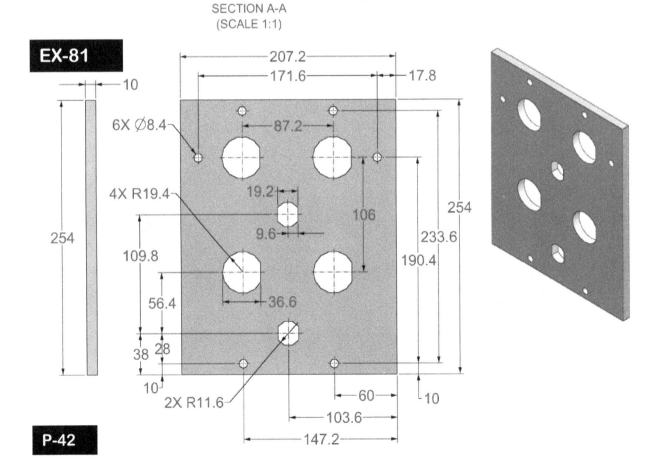

10

207.2

171.6

17.8

6X ∅8.4

87.2

4X R19.4

19.2

9.6

106

254

233.6

190.4

254

109.8

56.4

36.6

38 28

10

2X R11.6

60

10

103.6

147.2

EX-82

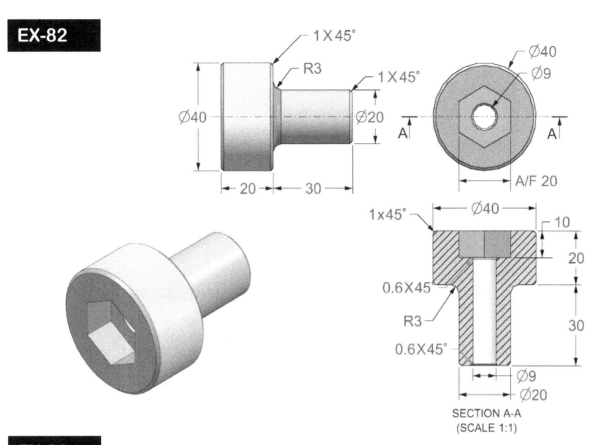

1 X 45°
R3
1 X 45°
Ø40
Ø20
20
30

Ø40
Ø9
A/F 20

1x45°
Ø40
10
20
0.6X45
R3
30
0.6X45°
Ø9
Ø20

SECTION A-A
(SCALE 1:1)

EX-83

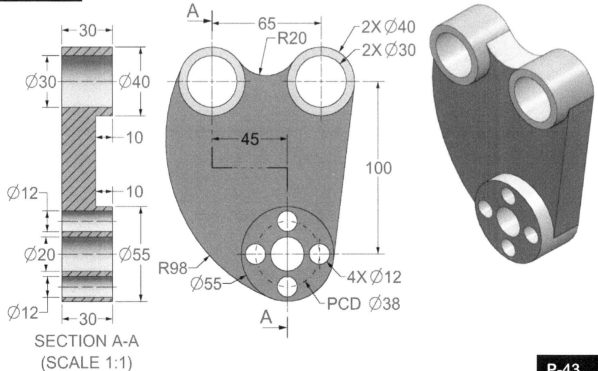

30
Ø30
Ø40
10
10
Ø12
Ø20
Ø55
Ø12
30

SECTION A-A
(SCALE 1:1)

A
65
R20
2X Ø40
2X Ø30
45
100
R98
Ø55
4X Ø12
PCD Ø38
A

EX-84

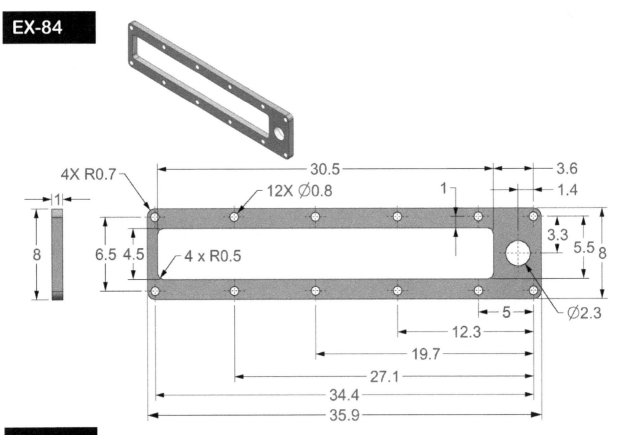

4X R0.7

12X Ø0.8

4 x R0.5

30.5

3.6

1.4

1

3.3

5.5

8

1

8

6.5 4.5

5

12.3

19.7

27.1

34.4

35.9

Ø2.3

EX-85

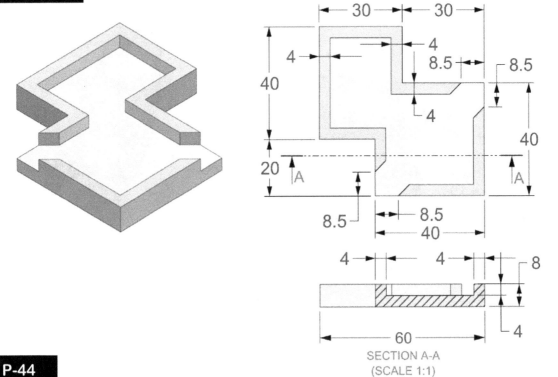

30

30

4

4

8.5

8.5

40

4

4

40

20

A

A

8.5

8.5

40

4

4

8

60

SECTION A-A
(SCALE 1:1)

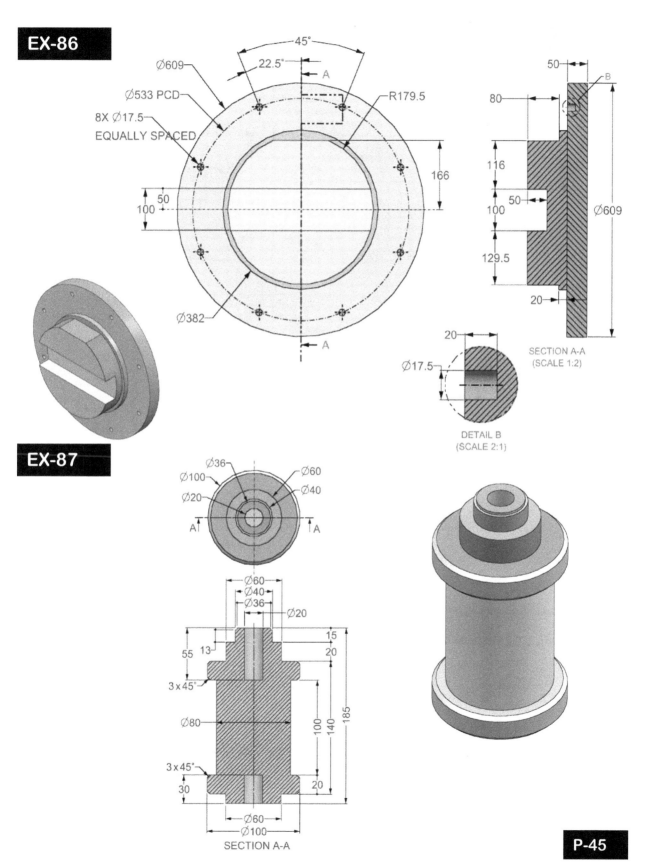

EX-86

Ø609
Ø533 PCD
8X Ø17.5
EQUALLY SPACED
45°
22.5°
A
R179.5
166
50
100
Ø382
A

50
80
B
116
100
50
129.5
20
Ø609

SECTION A-A
(SCALE 1:2)

20
Ø17.5

DETAIL B
(SCALE 2:1)

EX-87

Ø36
Ø100
Ø20
Ø60
Ø40
A   A

Ø60
Ø40
Ø36
Ø20
15
20
55   13
100
140
185
3 x 45°
Ø80
3 x 45°
20
30
Ø60
Ø100
SECTION A-A

P-45

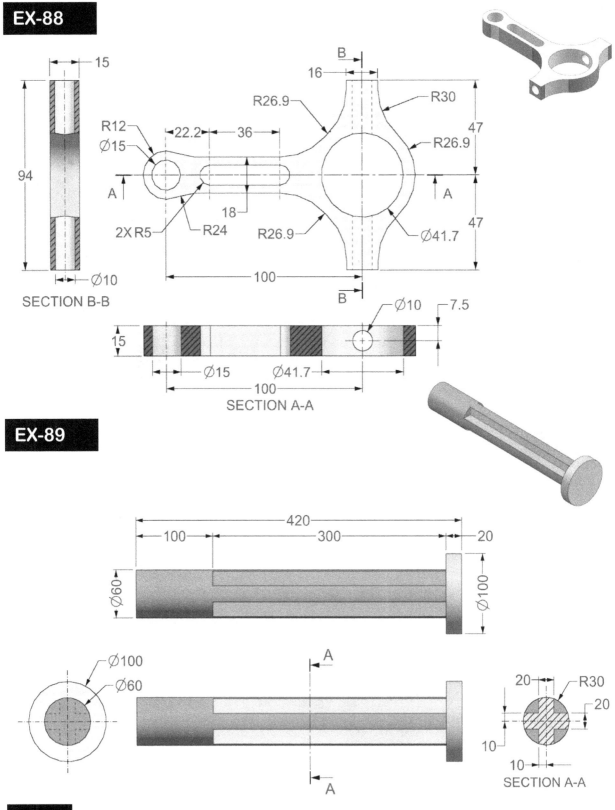

EX-88

R12
∅15
22.2
36
R26.9
R30
16
B
R30
47
R26.9
94
15
A
A
18
R24
2X R5
R26.9
∅41.7
R26.9
47
100
B

SECTION B-B
∅10

SECTION A-A
∅10
7.5
15
∅15
∅41.7
100

EX-89

420
100
300
20
∅60
∅100

∅100
∅60
A
A
20
R30
20
10
10
SECTION A-A

P-46

EX-90

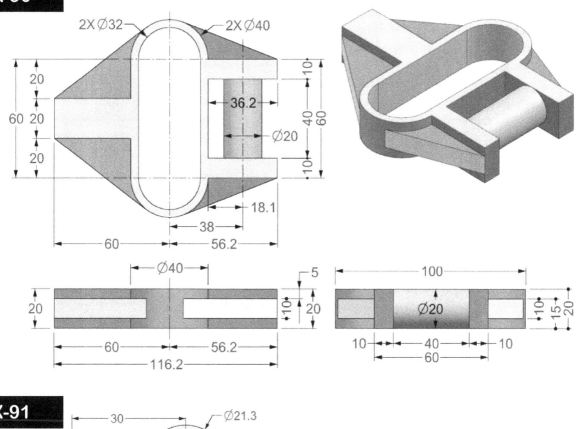

EX-91

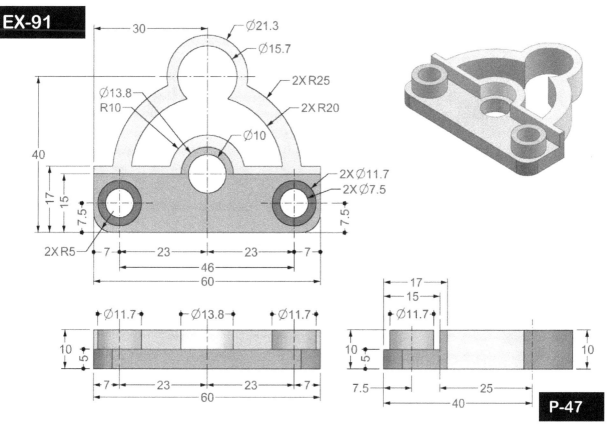

P-47

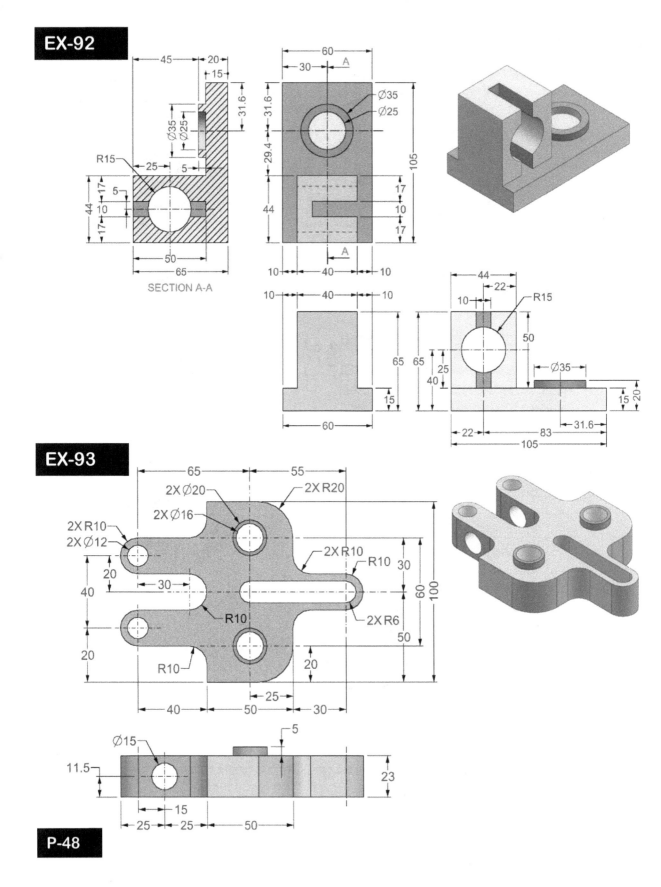

EX-92

SECTION A-A

EX-93

2X Ø20
2X R20
2X Ø16
2X R10
2X Ø12
2X R10
R10
2X R6
R10
R10
Ø15

P-48

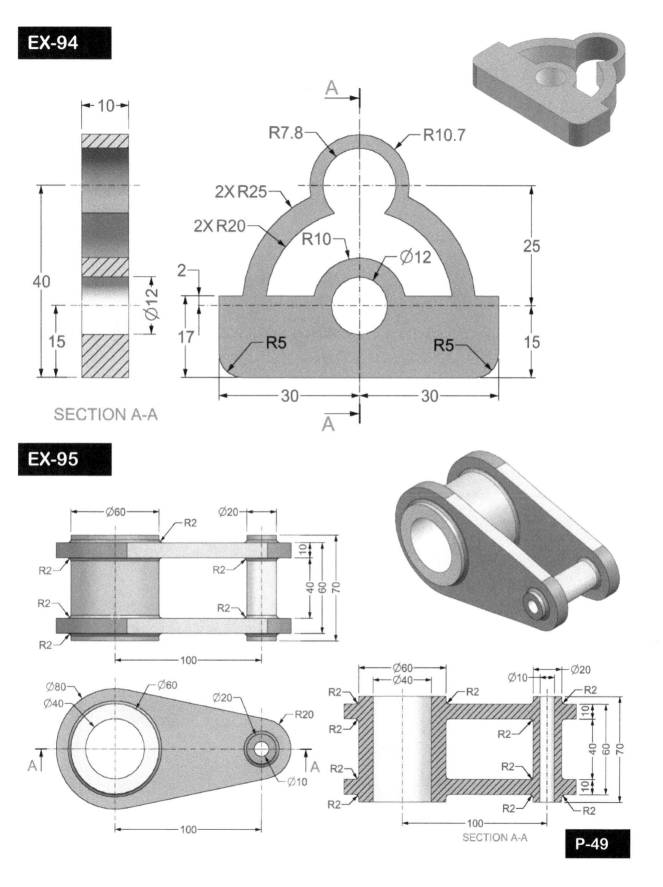

EX-94

SECTION A-A

10

40

15

Ø12

A

R7.8   R10.7

2X R25

2X R20

R10   Ø12

2

17

15

25

R5   R5

30   30

A

EX-95

Ø60   Ø20   R2

R2

R2   R2

R2   R2

R2   R2

10
40
60
70

100

Ø80   Ø60
Ø40   Ø20   R20

A   A

Ø10

100

Ø60
Ø40   Ø10   Ø20

R2   R2

R2   R2

R2   R2

R2   R2

R2   R2   R2

10
40
60
70

100

SECTION A-A

P-49

EX-96

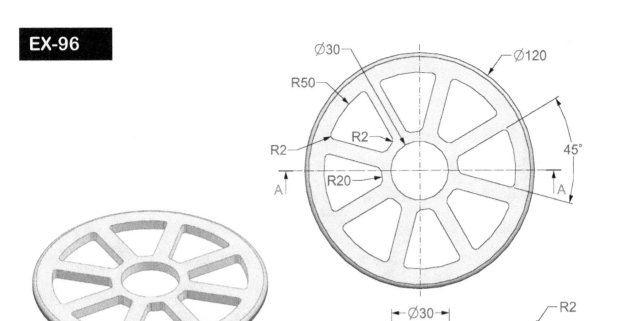

Ø30
Ø120
R50
R2
R2
R20
45°
Ø30
Ø120
R2
R2

SECTION A-A

EX-97

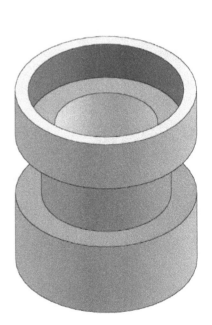

Ø70
Ø60
Ø40
A — A

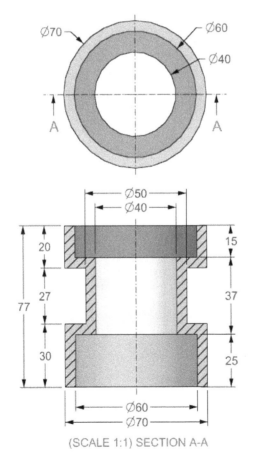

Ø50
Ø40
20
15
27
37
77
30
25
Ø60
Ø70

(SCALE 1:1) SECTION A-A

P-50

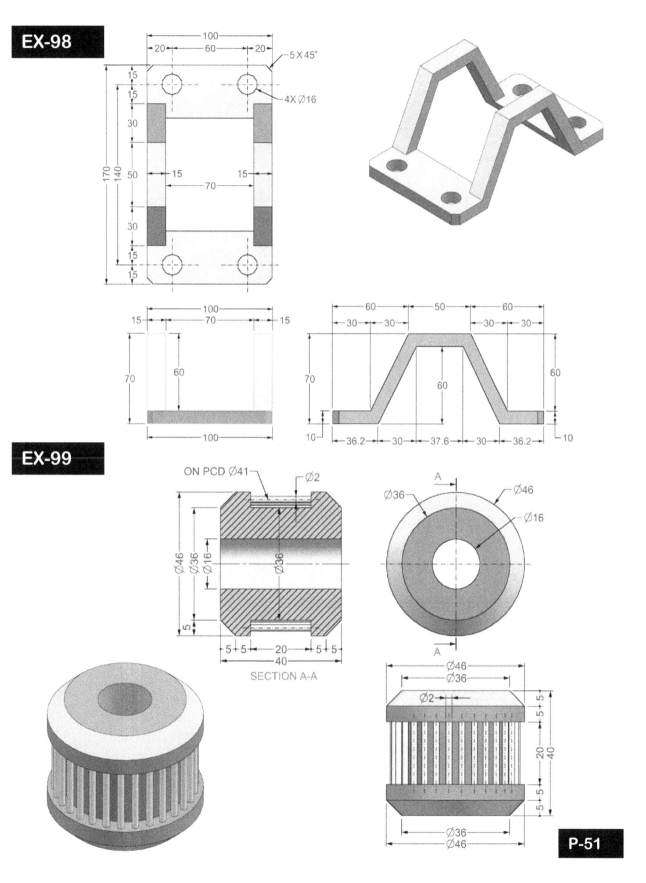

EX-98

100
20 60 20
5 X 45°
15
15
30
4X ∅16
170 140 50 15 15
70
30
15
15

100
15 70 15
70 60
100

60 50 60
30 30 30 30
70 60 60
10 36.2 30 37.6 30 36.2 10

EX-99

ON PCD ∅41 ∅2
∅46 ∅36 ∅16 ∅36
5
5 5 20 5 5
40
SECTION A-A

A
∅36 ∅46
∅16
A

∅46
∅36
∅2
5 5
5 5
20 40
5 5
5 5
∅36
∅46

P-51

EX-100

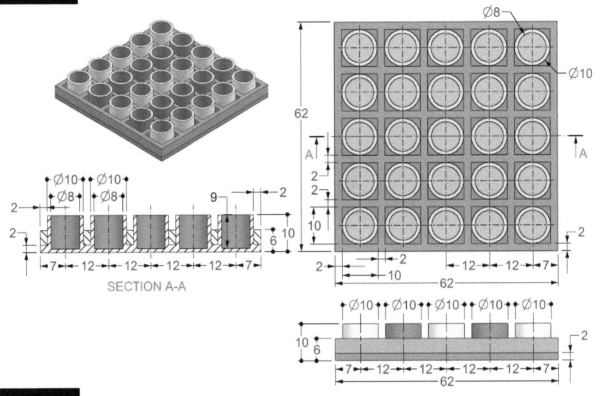

SECTION A-A

EX-101

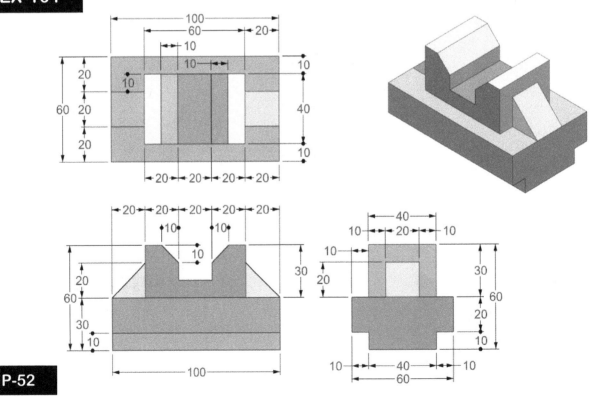

P-52

EX-102

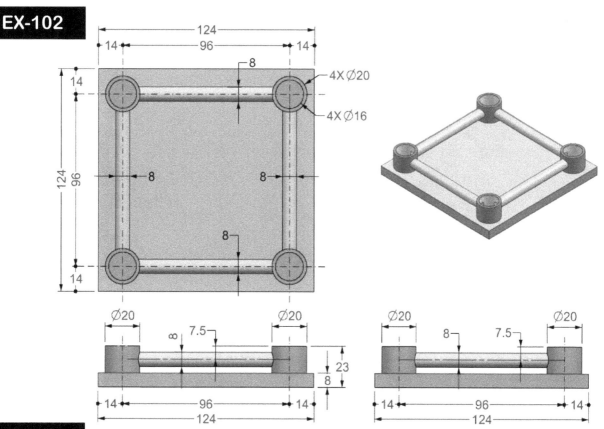

EX-103

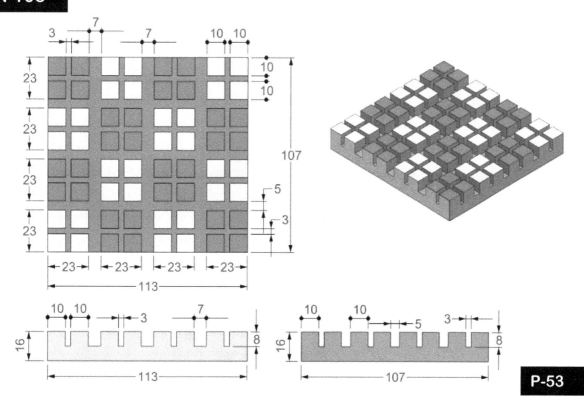

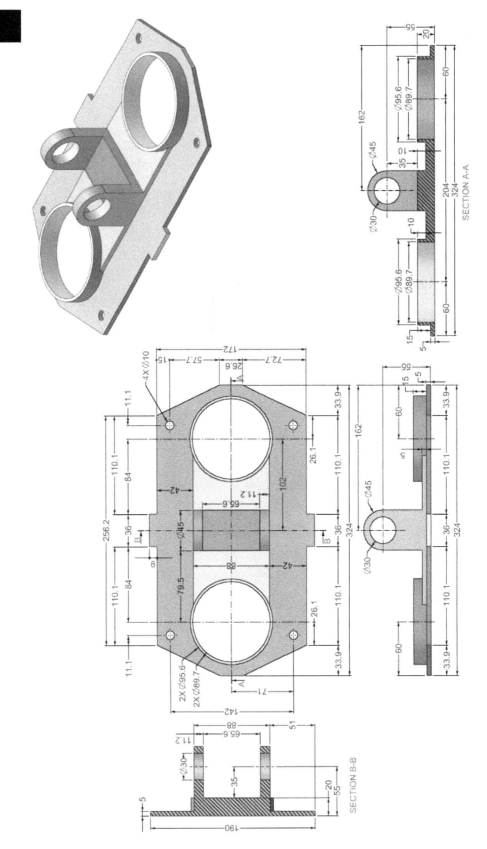

SECTION A-A

SECTION B-B

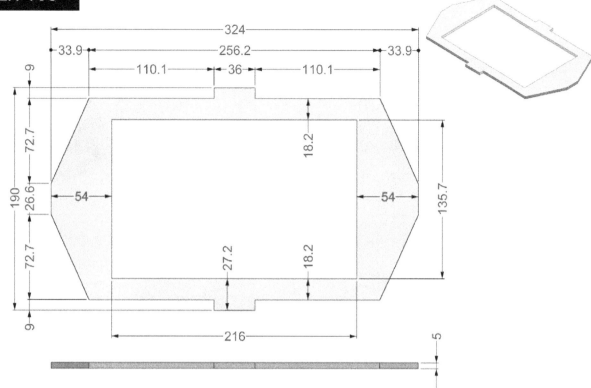

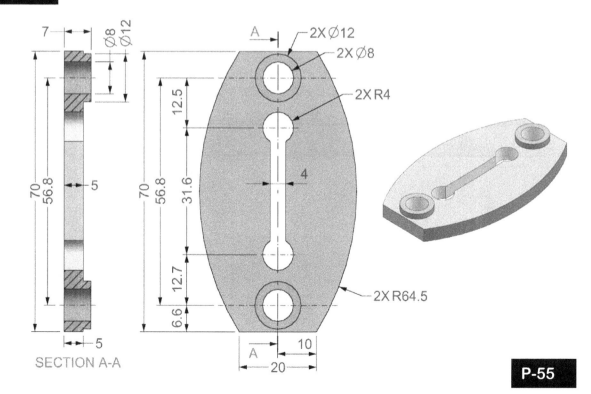

SECTION A-A

EX-107

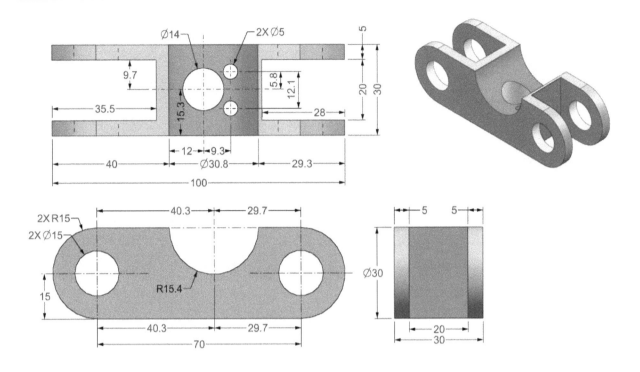

EX-108

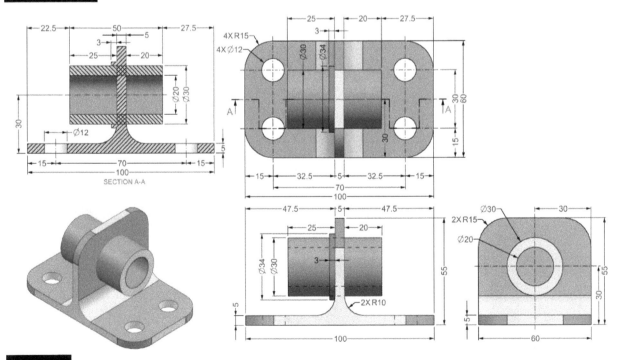

SECTION A-A

P-56

EX-109

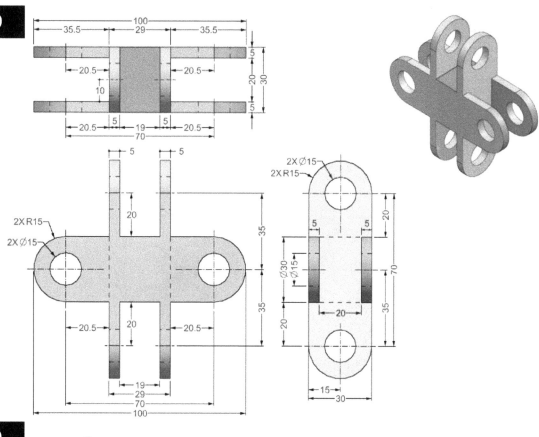

EX-110

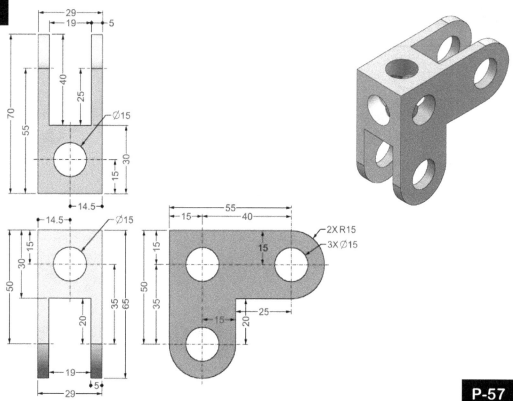

EX-111

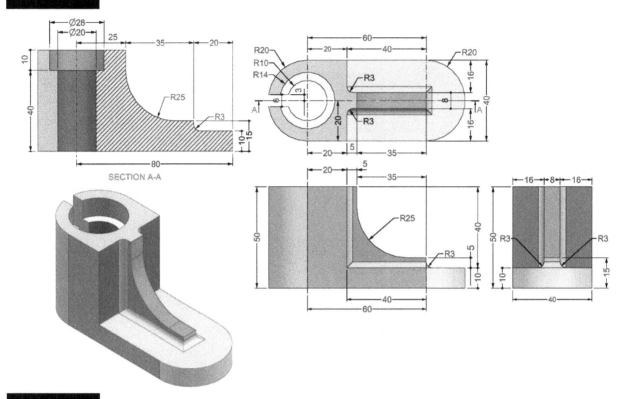

SECTION A-A

EX-112

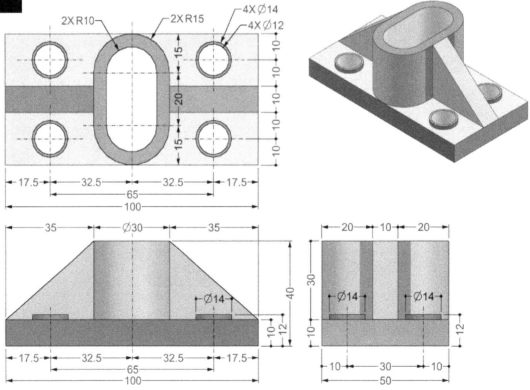

P-58

EX-113

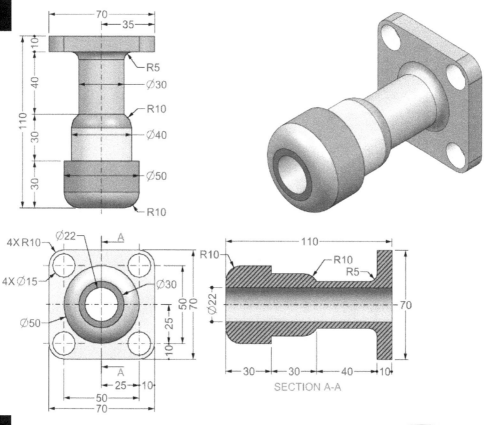

4X R10 Ø22
4X Ø15
Ø50
Ø30
50
70
25
10
25
10
50
70

R10
R10
R5
110
Ø22
70
30
30
40
10

SECTION A-A

EX-114

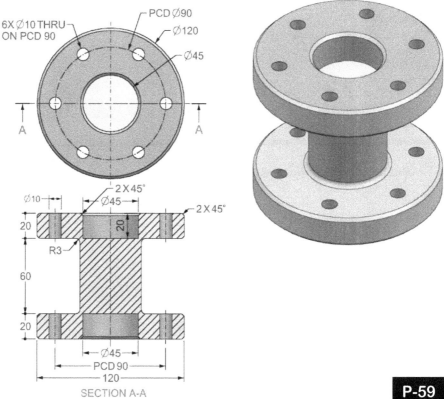

6X Ø10 THRU
ON PCD 90
PCD Ø90
Ø120
Ø45

A   A

Ø10
2 X 45°
Ø45
2 X 45°
20
20
R3
60
20
Ø45
PCD 90
120

SECTION A-A

EX-115

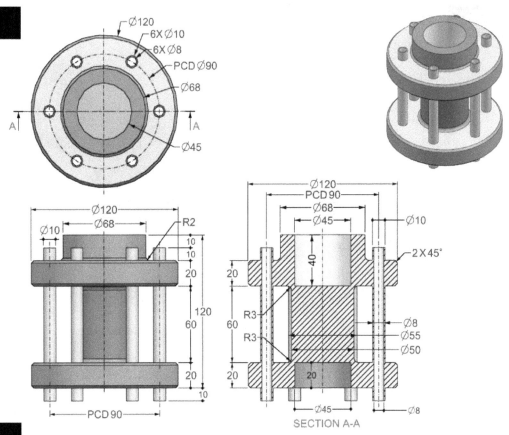

Ø120
6X Ø10
6X Ø8
PCD Ø90
Ø68
Ø45

A — A

Ø120
Ø68
Ø10
R2
10
10
20
120
60
20
10
PCD 90

Ø120
PCD 90
Ø68
Ø45
Ø10
20
40
2 X 45°
20
60
R3
R3
Ø8
Ø55
Ø50
20
Ø45
Ø8
SECTION A-A

EX-116

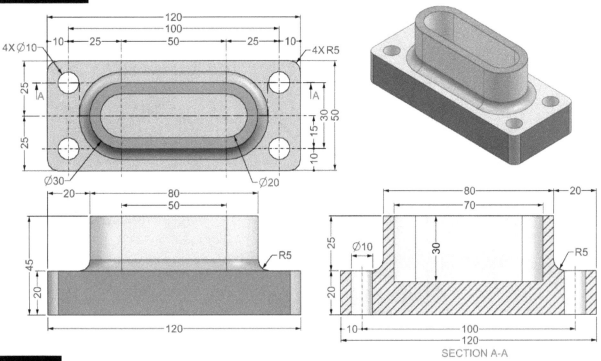

120
100
10
25
50
25
10
4X Ø10
4X R5
25
A — A
30
50
25
15
10
Ø30
Ø20

20
80
50
45
20
R5
120

80
20
70
25
Ø10
30
R5
10
100
120
SECTION A-A

P-60

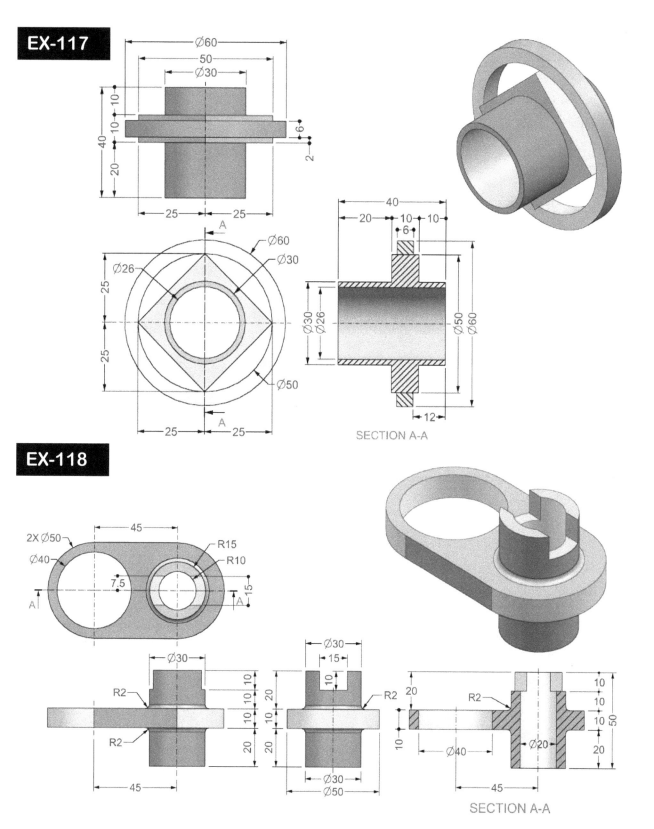

EX-117

Ø60
50
Ø30
10
10
40
20
25 25
6
2

A

Ø60
Ø30
Ø26
25
25
Ø50
25 25
A

40
20 10 10
6
Ø30
Ø26
Ø50
Ø60
12

SECTION A-A

EX-118

2X Ø50
Ø40
R15
R10
7.5
15
A A

45

Ø30
R2
R2
10 10 10 20
45

Ø30
15
10
20 10 20
R2
Ø30
Ø50

20
R2
Ø40
10
Ø20
45
10 10 10 50
20

SECTION A-A

P-61

EX-119

Ø190
Ø55

2X R20
2X R25
Ø140
70
A
R25

25
50
50
25

Ø55
Ø75
Ø100
Ø180
Ø190

A
Ø75
Ø190

SECTION A-A

Ø75
Ø190
Ø55
Ø180
Ø100

EX-120

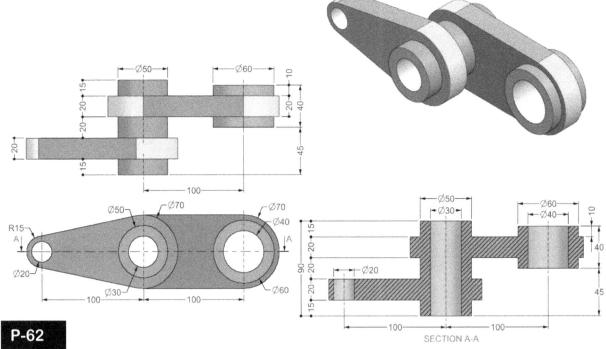

Ø50
Ø60
10
15
20
20
40
20
15
20
45
100

Ø50
Ø70
Ø70
Ø40
R15
A
A
Ø20
Ø30
Ø60
100
100

Ø50
Ø30
Ø60
Ø40
10
90
20
15
20
20
Ø20
40
15
20
45
100
100

SECTION A-A

P-62

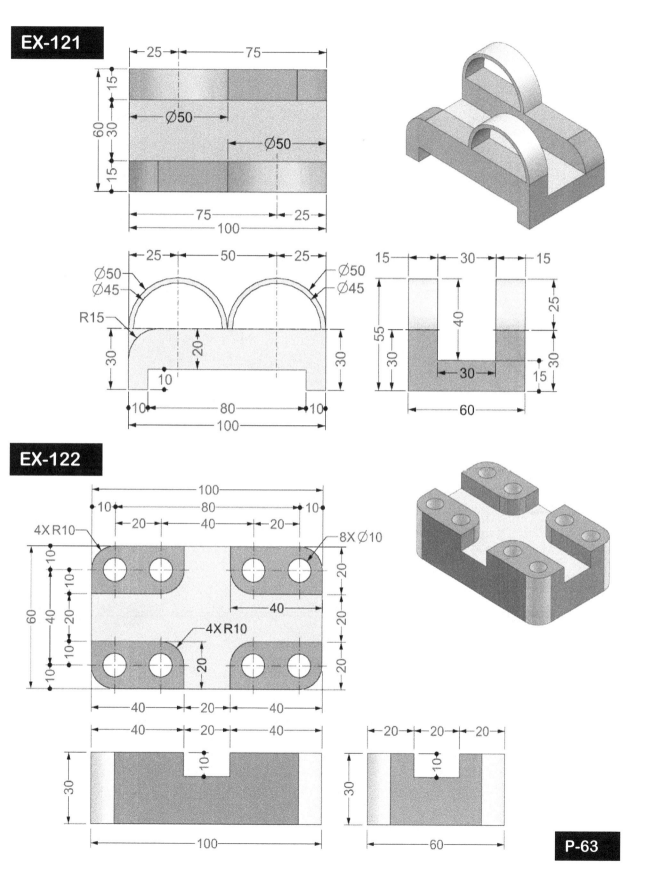

EX-121

EX-122

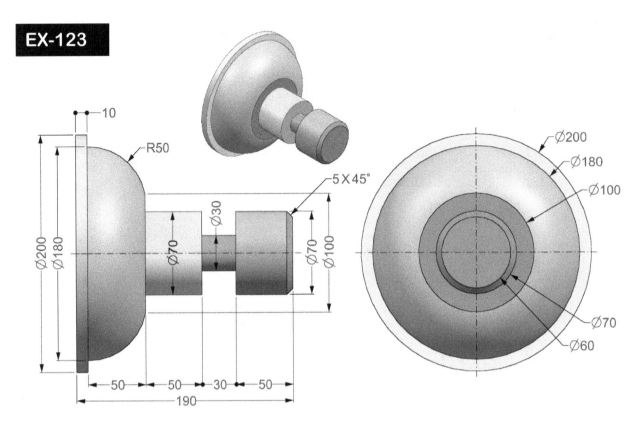

10
R50
Ø200
Ø180
Ø100
Ø70
Ø60
5 X 45°
Ø30
Ø70
Ø200
Ø180
Ø70
Ø100
50
50
30
50
190

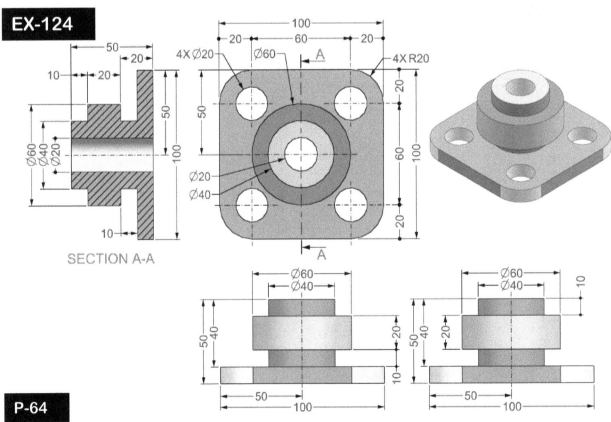

50
20
10
20
4X Ø20
Ø60
A
4X R20
100
20
60
20
20
50
50
60
20
100
Ø60
Ø40
Ø20
Ø20
Ø40
10
A
10
SECTION A-A

Ø60
Ø40
Ø60
Ø40
50
40
20
10
10
20
50
40
50
50
100
100

EX-125

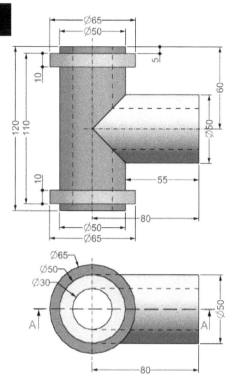

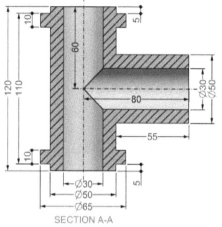

SECTION A-A

EX-126

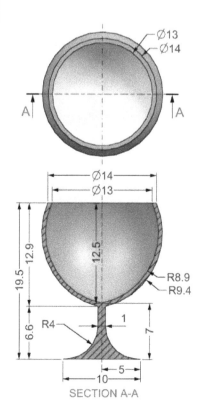

SECTION A-A

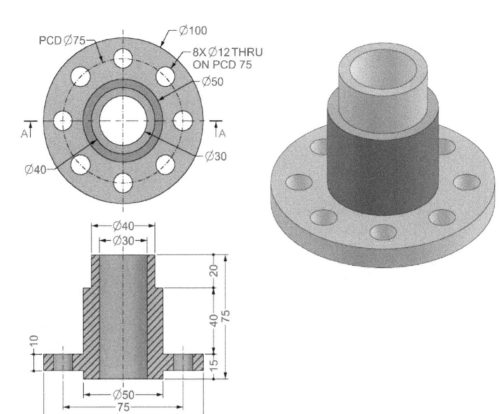

PCD Ø75
Ø100
8X Ø12 THRU
ON PCD 75
Ø50
A
A
Ø40
Ø30

Ø40
Ø30
20
40
75
10
15
Ø50
75
Ø100
SECTION A-A

EX-128

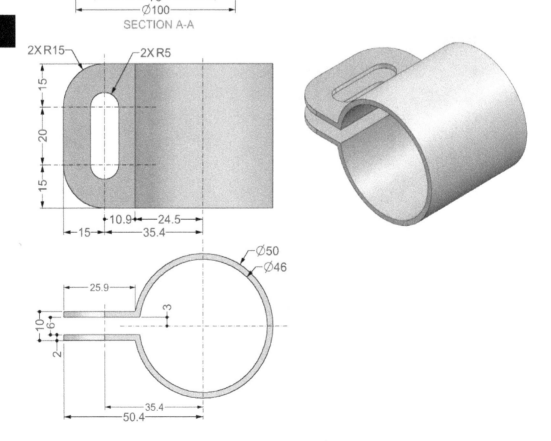

2X R15
2X R5
15
20
15
10.9
24.5
15
35.4

Ø50
Ø46
25.9
3
10
6
2
35.4
50.4

EX-129

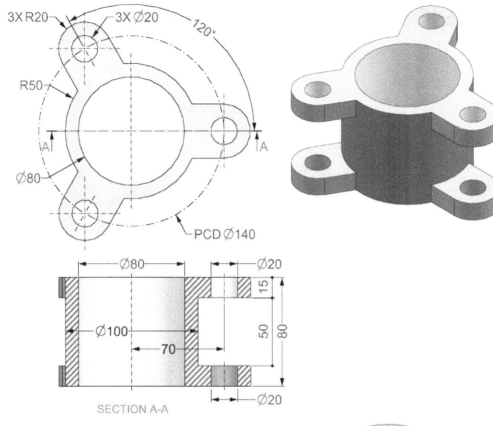

3X R20   3X Ø20   120°

R50

A   A

Ø80

PCD Ø140

Ø80   Ø20

15

Ø100   50   80

70

Ø20

SECTION A-A

EX-130

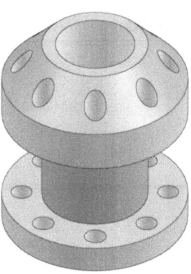

PCD Ø55   Ø70

A   A

8X Ø8
ON PCD 55
Ø30   Ø40

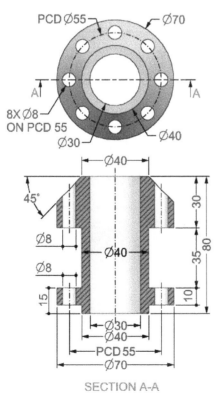

Ø40

45°   30

Ø8   80

Ø40

Ø8   35

15   10

Ø30
Ø40
PCD 55
Ø70

SECTION A-A

EX-131

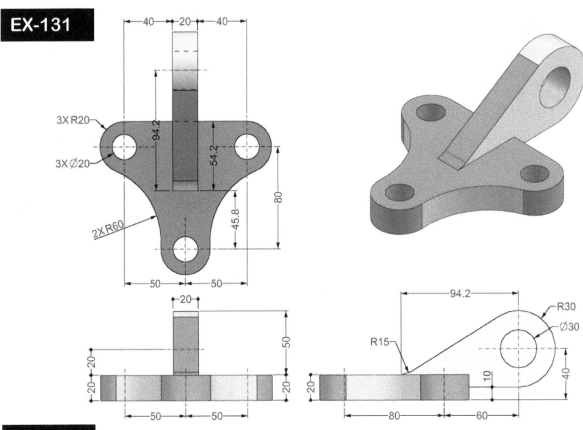

EX-132

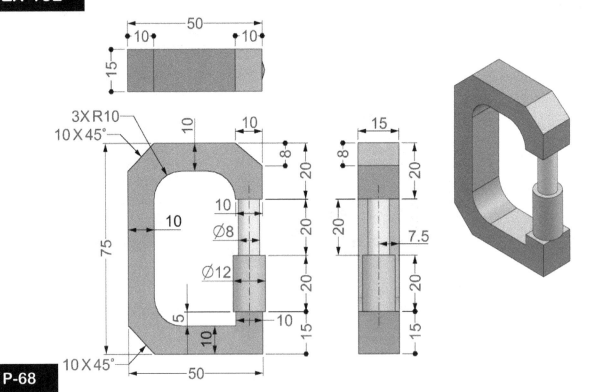

P-68

EX-133

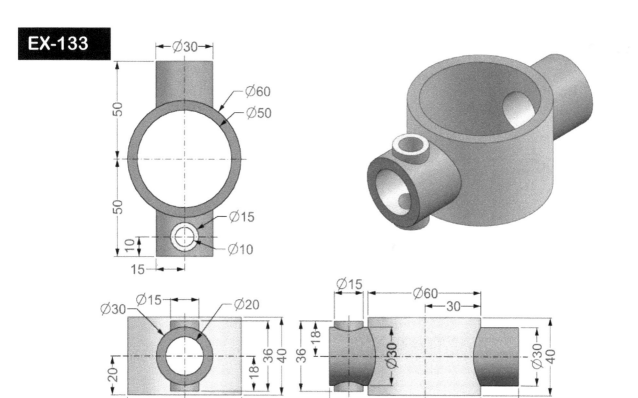

EX-134

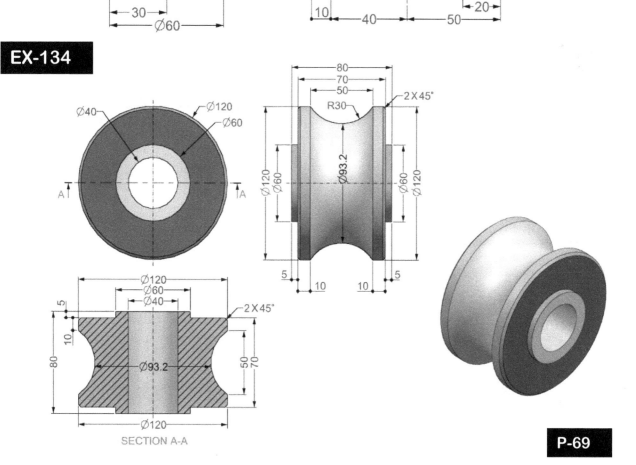

SECTION A-A

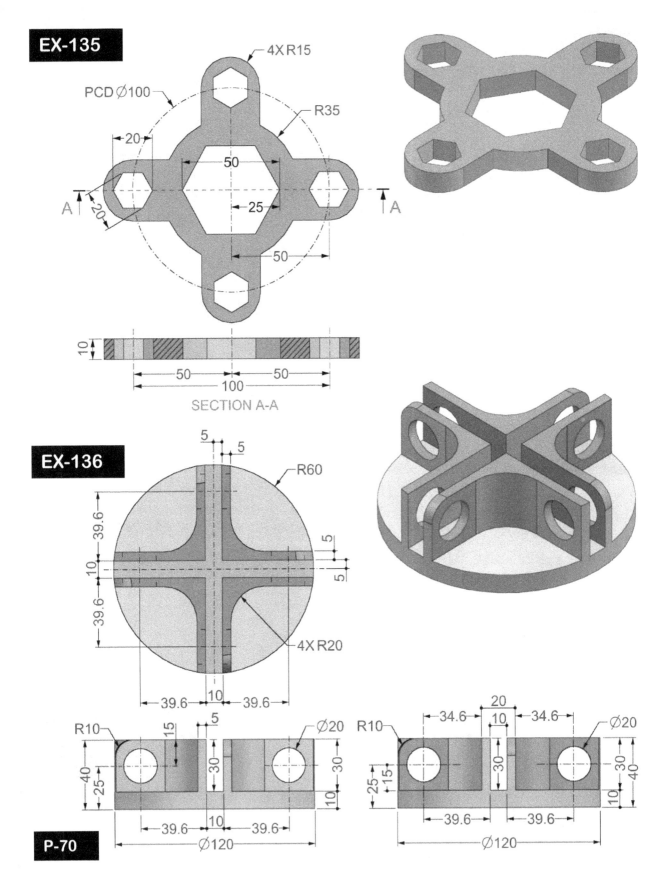

EX-135

4X R15

PCD ⌀100

R35

20

50

25

50

A

20

A

10

50

50

100

SECTION A-A

EX-136

5

5

R60

39.6

10

5

39.6

5

4X R20

39.6

10

39.6

R10

15

5

⌀20

40

25

30

30

39.6

10

39.6

⌀120

20

R10

34.6

10

34.6

⌀20

25

15

30

30

40

10

39.6

39.6

⌀120

P-70

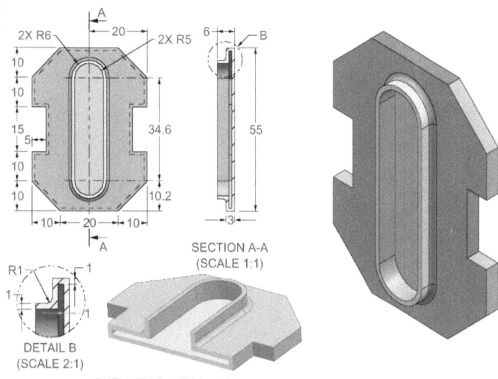

2X R6
2X R5
20
A
B
6
10
10
15
5
10
10
34.6
55
10.2
3
10
20
10

A

SECTION A-A
(SCALE 1:1)

R1
1
1
1
1

DETAIL B
(SCALE 2:1)

SHELL THICKNESS = 1MM
ALL INSIDE WALL THICKNESS

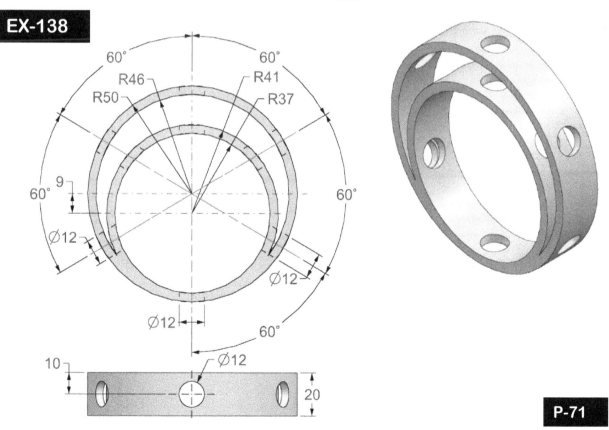

60°
60°
R46
R41
R50
R37
60°
60°
9
Ø12
Ø12
Ø12
60°
Ø12
10
Ø12
20

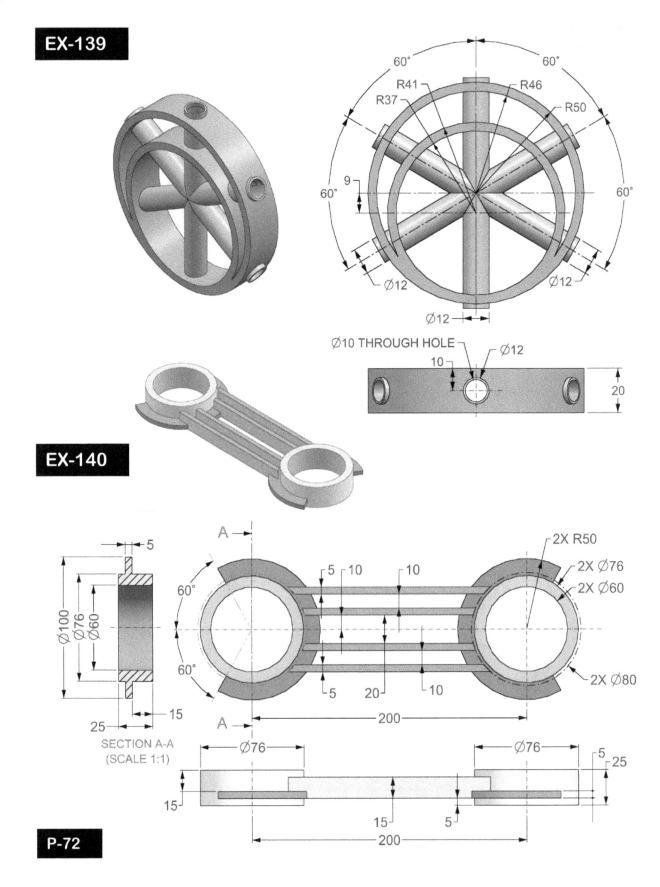

EX-139

R41
R46
R37
R50
60° 60°
60° 60°
60° 60°
9
Ø12
Ø12
Ø12

Ø10 THROUGH HOLE
Ø12
10
20

EX-140

A

2X R50
2X Ø76
2X Ø60

5 10 10
60°

60°

5
Ø100
Ø76
Ø60

5 20 10

2X Ø80

15
25

SECTION A-A
(SCALE 1:1)

A

200

Ø76
Ø76
5
25
15
15 5
200

P-72

EX-141

Ø100
Ø60
Ø6
Ø120

Ø60
Ø6
R5
30
R40.7
10
10
100
50
Ø60
R5
R2 R5
20
Ø80
30
Ø120

EX-142

18
14
15
41.4
15.4
R15
R10
Ø8
46.8
Ø16.2
8
23.4
Ø20.4
26
Ø16.2
R6

10 20
15
5

P-73

EX-143

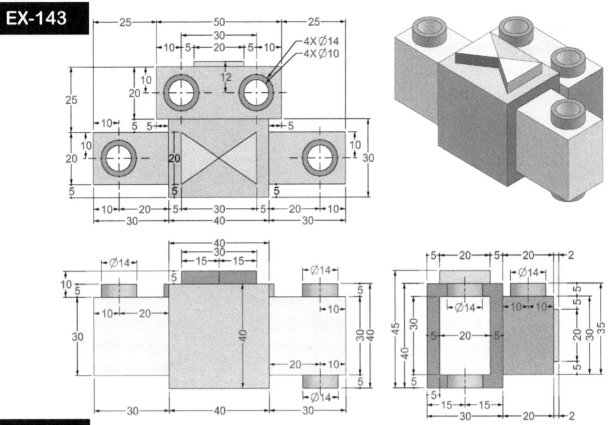

EX-144

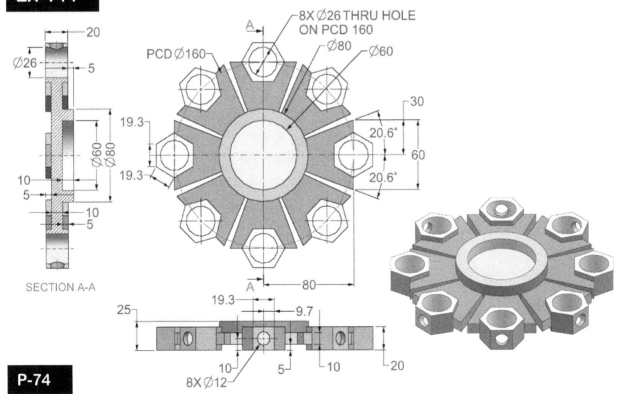

8X Ø26 THRU HOLE ON PCD 160

PCD Ø160

SECTION A-A

8X Ø12

P-74

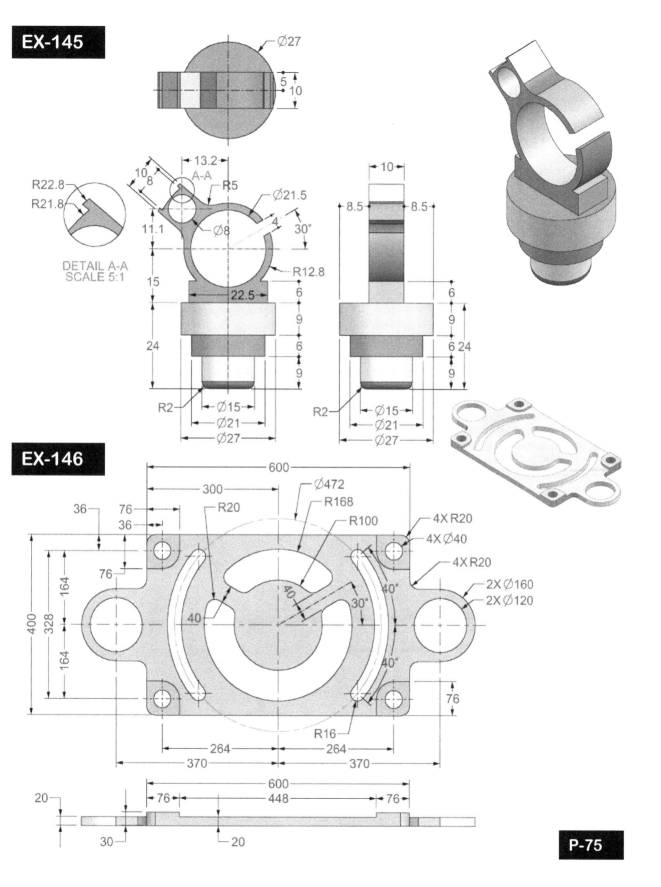

EX-145

Ø27

5
10

DETAIL A-A
SCALE 5:1

R22.8
R21.8

13.2
10
8
A-A
R5
Ø21.5
11.1
Ø8
4
30°
R12.8
15
22.5
6
9
24
6
9
R2
Ø15
Ø21
Ø27

10
8.5
8.5
6
9
6 24
9
R2
Ø15
Ø21
Ø27

EX-146

600
300
Ø472
R168
R100
36
76
4X R20
36
4X Ø40
76
4X R20
164
2X Ø160
400
328
40
2X Ø120
164
40
30°
40°
40°
76
264
264
R16
370
370

600
20
76
448
76
30
20

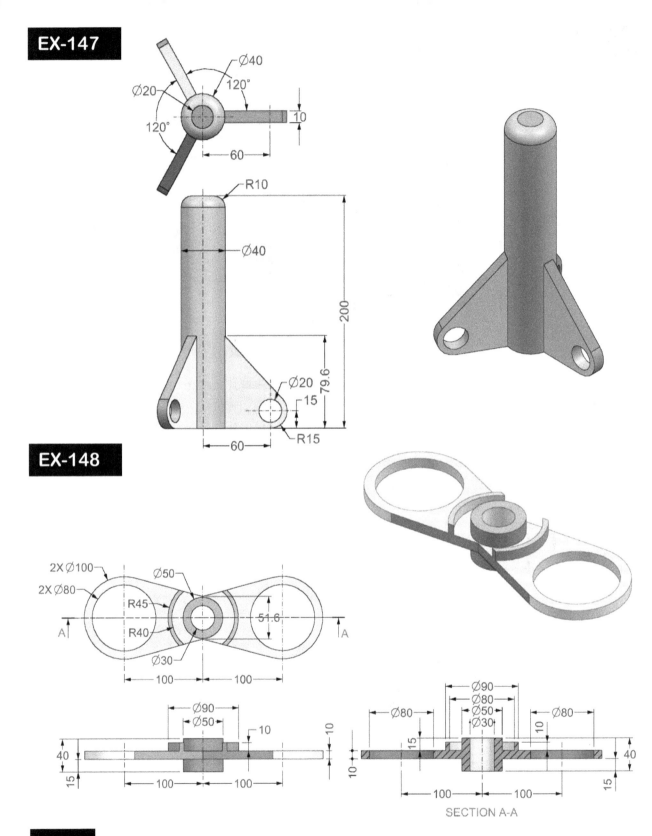

EX-147

Ø40
Ø20
120°
120°
10
60

R10
Ø40
200
79.6
Ø20
15
60
R15

EX-148

2X Ø100
2X Ø80
Ø50
R45
R40
Ø30
A
51.6
A
100
100

Ø90
Ø50
10
10
40
15
100
100

Ø90
Ø80
Ø50
Ø30
Ø80
Ø80
10
15
10
40
15
100
100

SECTION A-A

EX-149

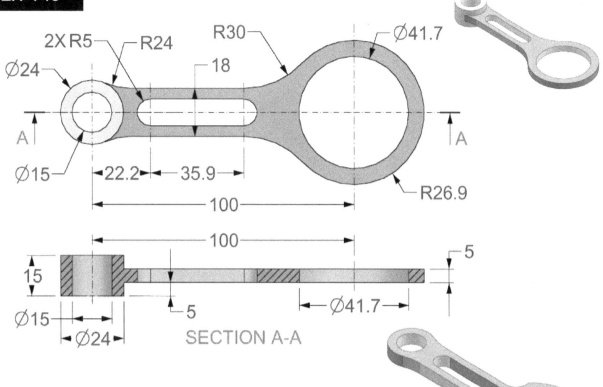

2X R5 — R24 — R30 — Ø41.7

Ø24

18

A

Ø15

22.2 — 35.9

100

R26.9

100

15

5

Ø15

Ø24

5

Ø41.7

SECTION A-A

EX-150

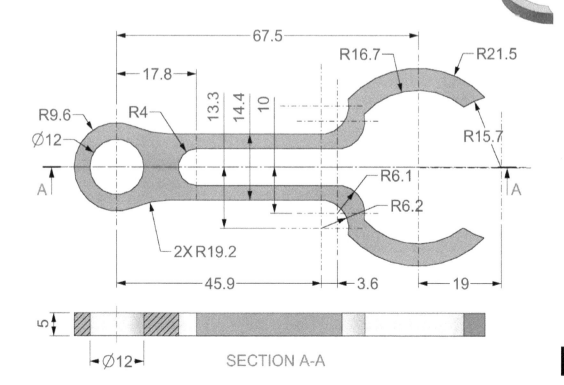

67.5

17.8

R16.7 — R21.5

R9.6

R4

13.3 14.4 10

R15.7

Ø12

A

R6.1

R6.2

2X R19.2

45.9

3.6

19

5

Ø12

SECTION A-A

EX-151

Ø8
6,5
10
28
R1.5
R1.5
1:1
B-B
27
Ø10

SECTION A-A

Ø20
A
R3
35
15°
20
5
A
Ø13.3
Ø16

R8
R10
R6.7
R4
R5

DETAIL B-B
SCALE 5:1
1
45°

EX-152

Ø20
Ø36
Ø58
Ø52
Ø16

Ø36
Ø20
R8
8
20
2
135°
13.5
R11.2
Ø16
15.8
76
10.7
21.6
13
10
R6
Ø16
R3

SECTION A-A

A
58
3
R3
R2
Ø52
76
R6
A
40

P-78

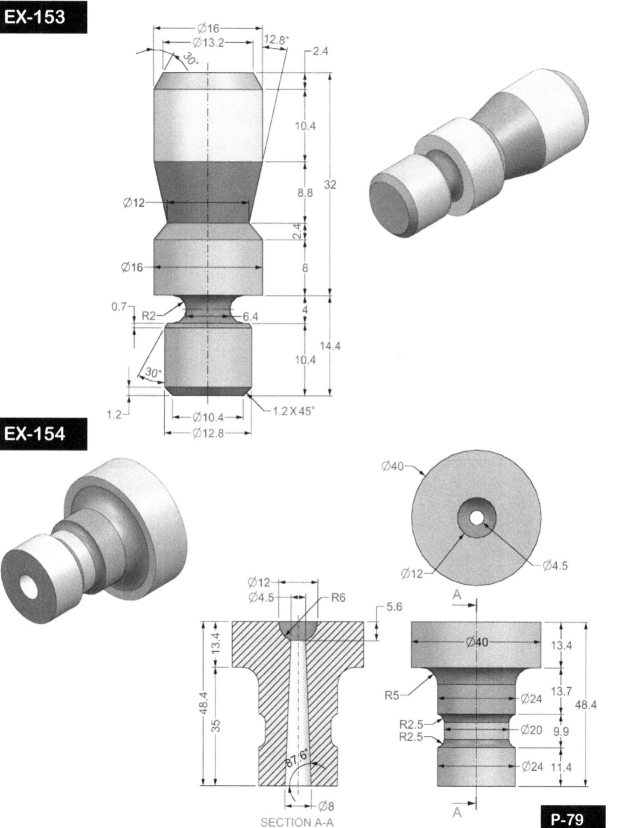

EX-153

⌀16
⌀13.2
12.8°
30°
2.4
10.4
32
8.8
2.4
⌀12
⌀16
8
0.7
R2
6.4
4
14.4
10.4
30°
1.2
⌀10.4
⌀12.8
1.2 X 45°

EX-154

⌀40
⌀12
⌀4.5

A

⌀12
⌀4.5
R6
5.6
13.4
⌀40
13.4
R5
⌀24
13.7
48.4
35
R2.5
⌀20
9.9
48.4
R2.5
⌀24
11.4
87.6°
⌀8
SECTION A-A
A

P-79

EX-155

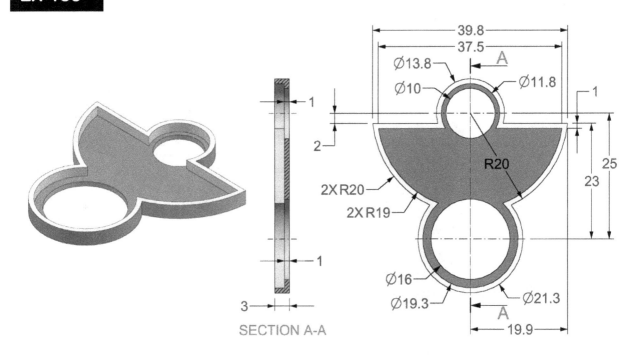

Ø13.8
Ø10
Ø11.8
39.8
37.5
A
R20
25
23
2X R20
2X R19
Ø16
Ø19.3
Ø21.3
A
19.9
1
2
1
3
SECTION A-A

EX-156

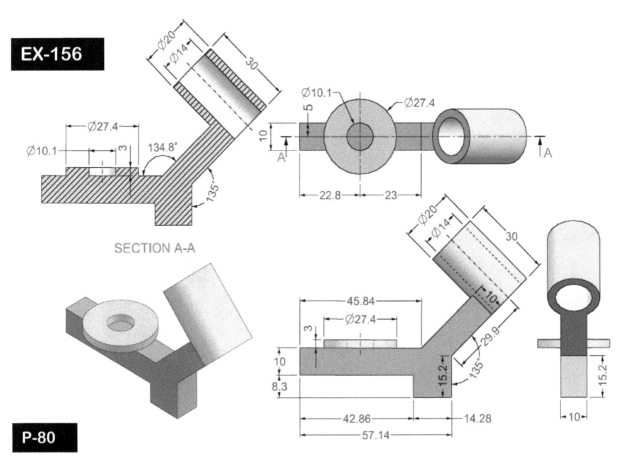

Ø20
Ø14
30
Ø27.4
Ø10.1
3
134.8°
135°
Ø10.1
10
5
Ø27.4
A
A
22.8
23
45.84
Ø27.4
3
10
8.3
15.2
135°
29.9
10
42.86
14.28
57.14
Ø20
Ø14
30
10
15.2
10

SECTION A-A

P-80

EX-157

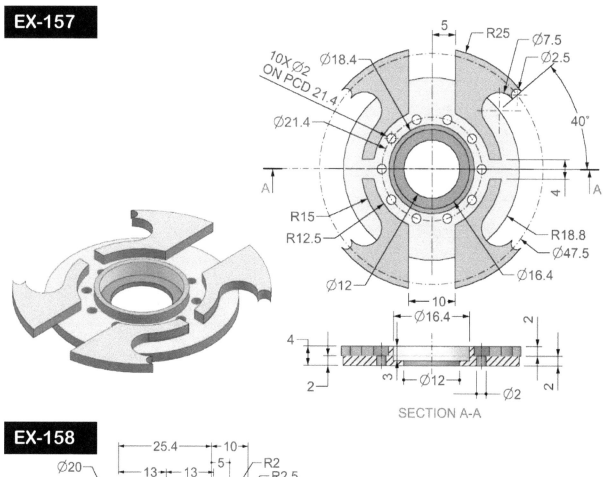

SECTION A-A

EX-158

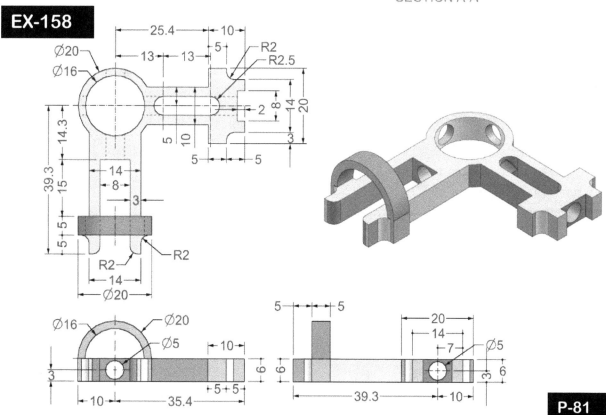

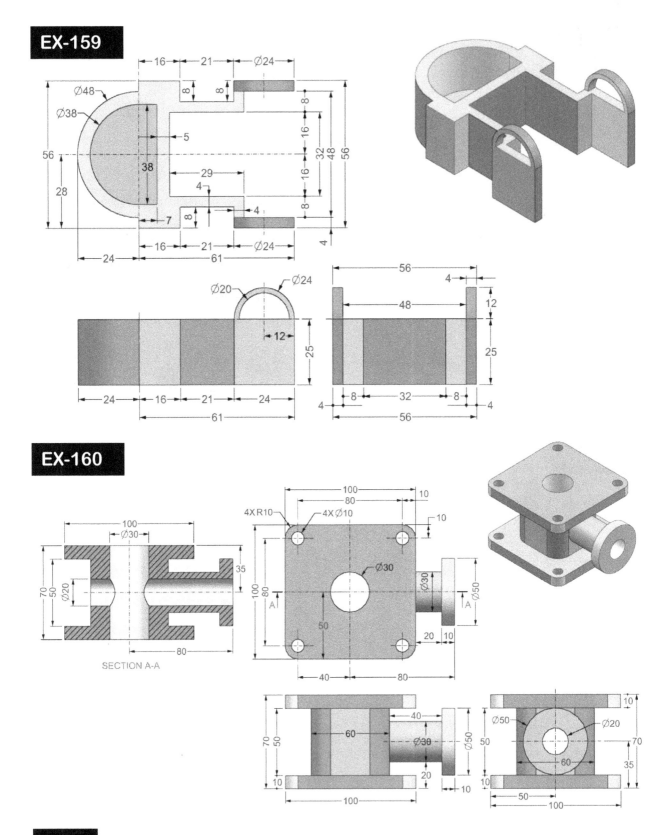

EX-159

EX-160

SECTION A-A

4X R10
4X Ø10

P-82

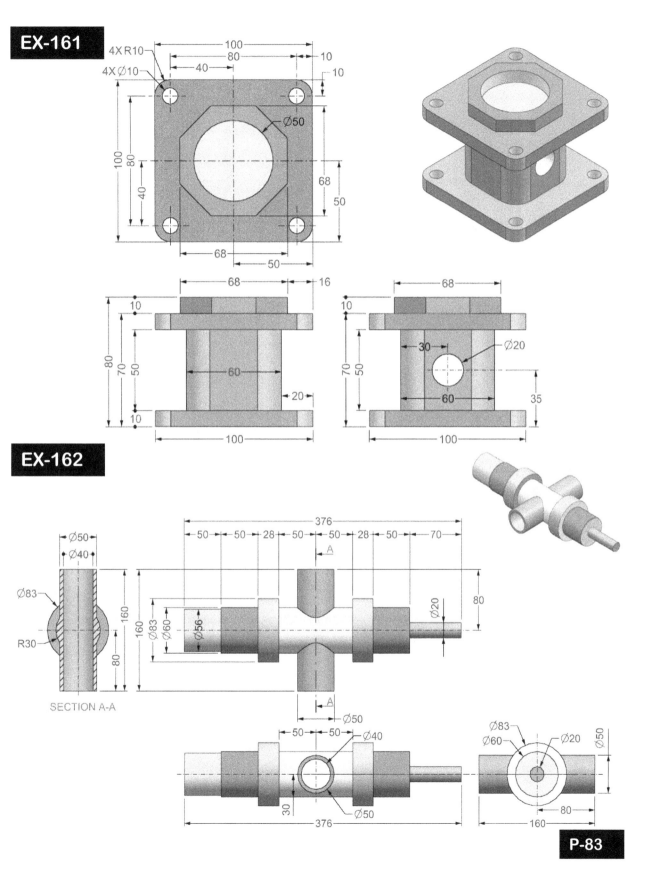

EX-161

4X R10
4X Ø10
100
80
40
10
10
Ø50
100
80
40
68
50
68
50

68
16
10
80
70
50
60
20
10
100

68
10
70
50
30
Ø20
60
35
100

EX-162

Ø50
Ø40
Ø83
R30
SECTION A-A

376
50 50 28 50 50 28 50 70
A
160
160
Ø83
Ø60
Ø56
80
Ø20
A

Ø50
50 50
Ø40
30
Ø50
376

Ø83
Ø60
Ø20
Ø50
80
160

P-83

EX-163

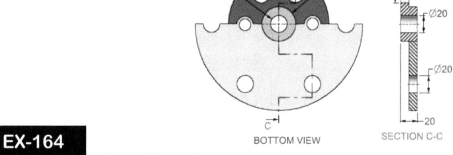

10

Ø20

Ø20

Ø20

20 — 10

SECTION A-A

PCD Ø160
4X Ø20
2X Ø20
2X R10

A

R100

Ø40

B   B

Ø20
PCD Ø80.5
Ø120

2X Ø14 THRU HOLES

A

TOP VIEW

10

Ø10

20

SECTION B-B

C

Ø20   Ø40

BOTTOM VIEW

C

10

Ø20

Ø20

Ø20

20

SECTION C-C

EX-164

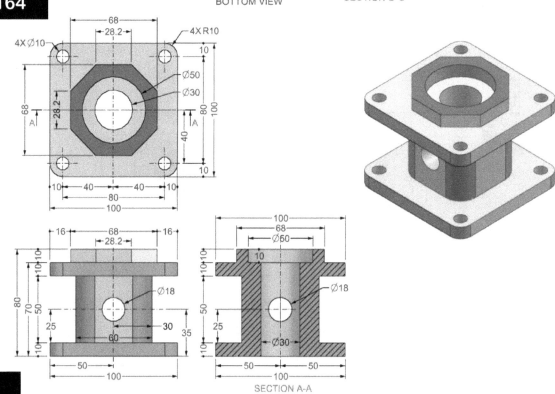

68
28.2
4X R10
4X Ø10

10

Ø50
Ø30

68   80   100

28.2
40
A   A

10

10   40   40   10
80
100

16   68   16
28.2
10 10
80
70
50
25
10
Ø18
30
60
50
100

100
68
Ø50
10 10
10
50
25
10
Ø18
35
Ø30
50   50
100
SECTION A-A

P-84

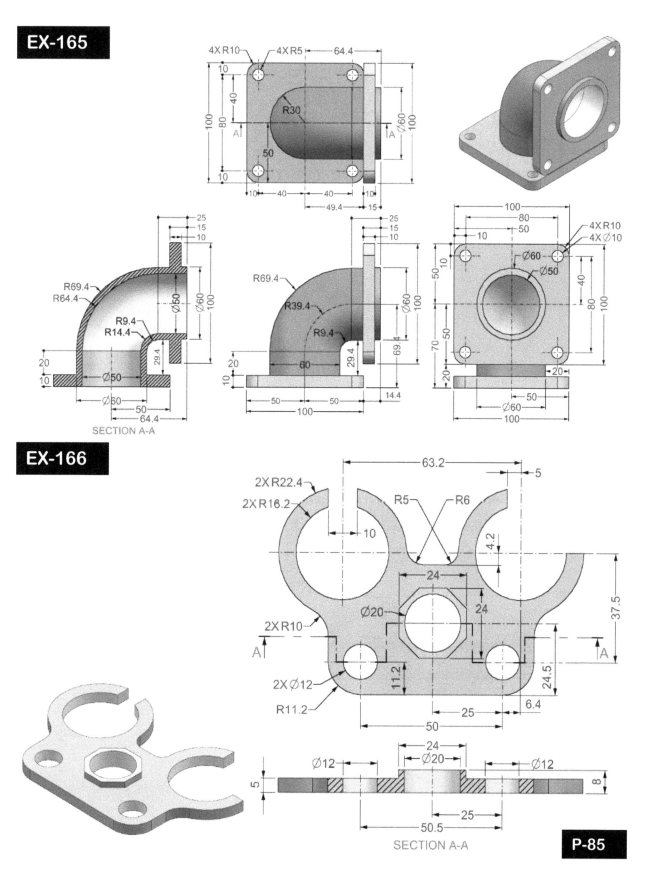

EX-165

EX-166

SECTION A-A

SECTION A-A

P-85

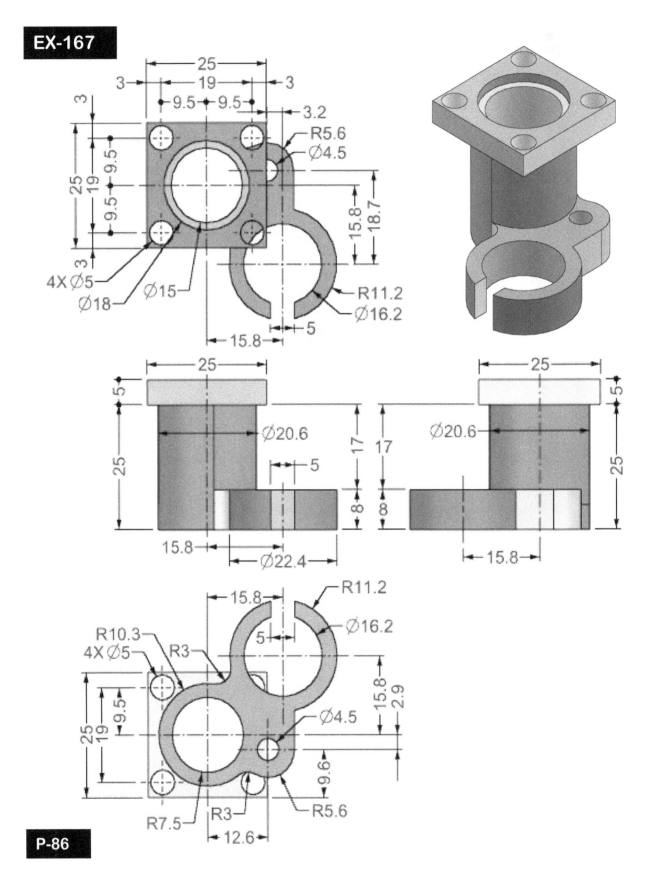

EX-167

P-86

EX-168

PCD Ø95
Ø120
8X Ø14
8X Ø10
ON PCD 95
R35
R25

A
A

32
30
80 16
32
20
2
Ø70
Ø120

30
Ø14
Ø10
16 20
Ø50
Ø70
PCD 95
Ø120

SECTION A-A

EX-169

Ø70
Ø40
20
40
R5
Ø28
Ø40

50
130
70
200

Ø70
R2
R60
Ø80
R5

30
40
140 80
30

21.3
50
Ø28
Ø40

10

50
80
70

Ø70
15 40 15
10
30
30
80
Ø28
Ø40
15
15
70
30
10
35
Ø70

6
3

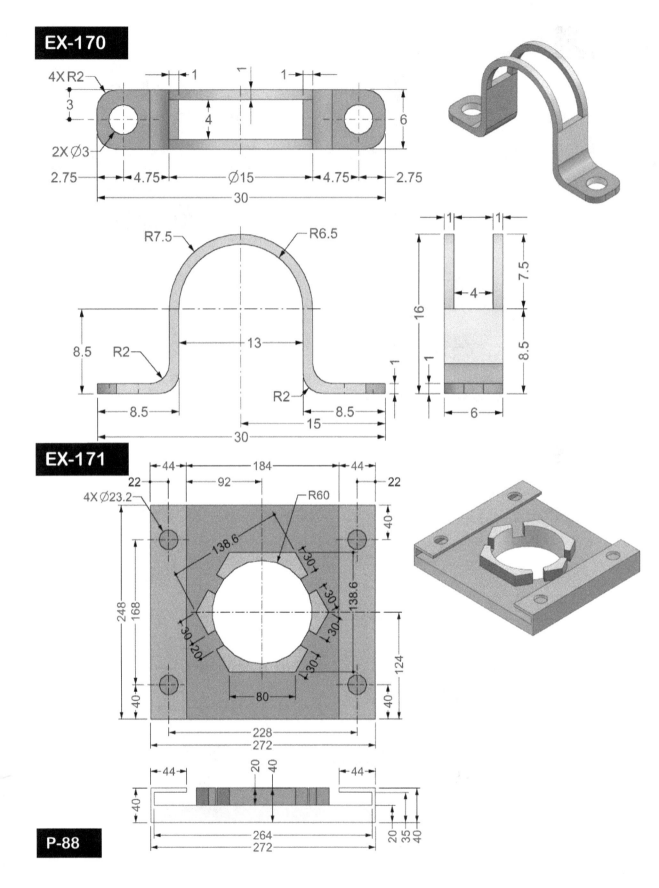

EX-170

4X R2
3
2X Ø3
2.75 — 4.75 — Ø15 — 4.75 — 2.75
30
1 — 1 — 1
4
6

R7.5 — R6.5
R2
8.5
13
R2
8.5 — 15 — 8.5
30

1 — 1
7.5
16 — 4
1 — 8.5
6

EX-171

44 — 184 — 44
22 — 92 — 22
4X Ø23.2 — R60
40
138.6 — 30
30
248 — 168 — 138.6
30 — 30
30 — 20
30
80 — 30
124
40 — 40
228
272

44 — 20 40 — 44
40 — 20 35 40
264
272

P-88

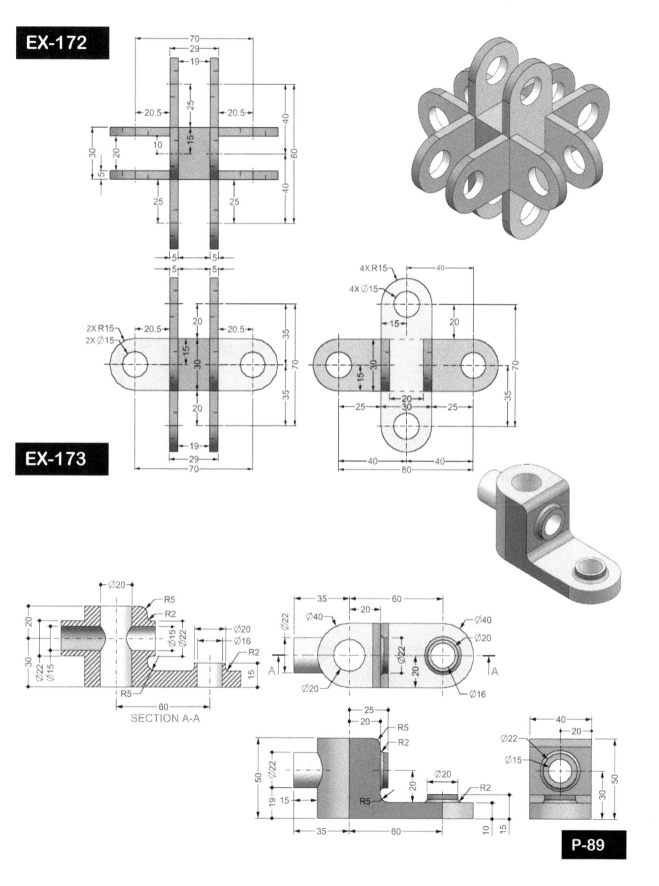

EX-172

EX-173

SECTION A-A

P-89

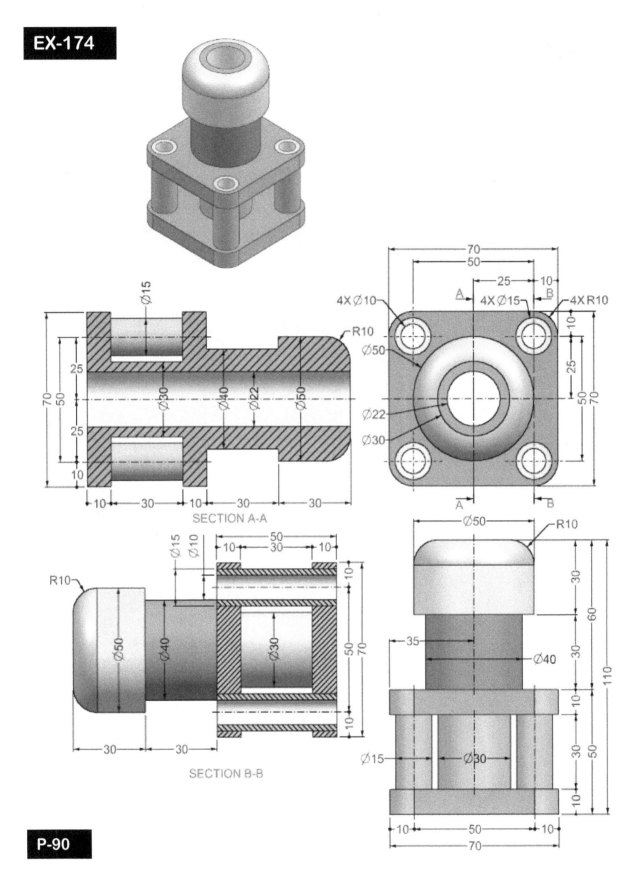

SECTION A-A

SECTION B-B

4X R10

70

35 35

10 25 25 10

4X Ø15

4X Ø10

Ø30

Ø22

10

35

25

70

A A

25

35

10

Ø30

Ø15 Ø15

20

10 5

10

30

50

Ø15 Ø15

30

50

50

70

10

Ø30

Ø22

Ø15
Ø10

20

30

70

10 5

10

30

Ø22

25 25

50

70

10

SECTION A-A

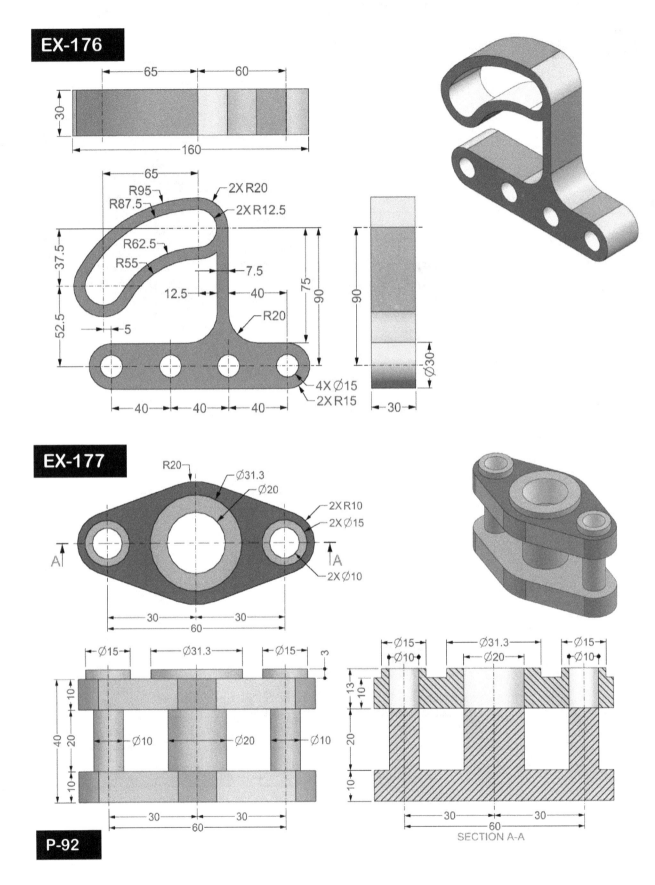

EX-176

EX-177

P-92

SECTION A-A

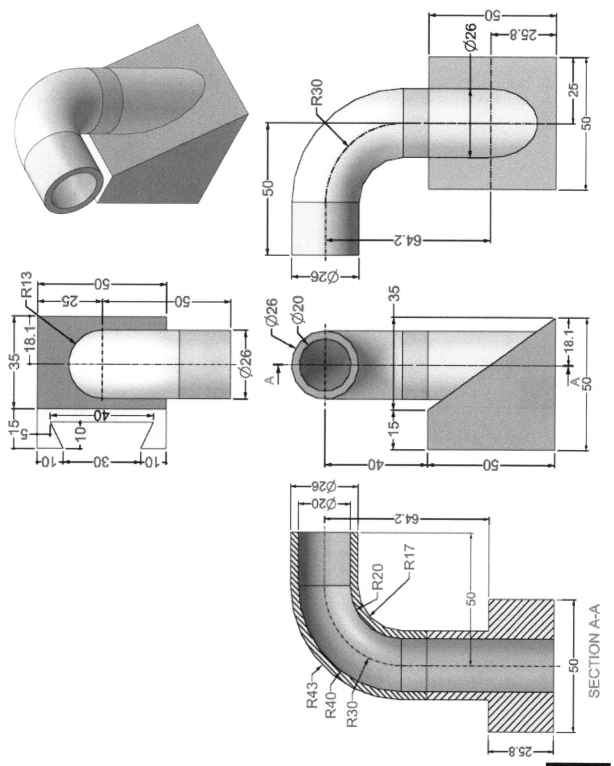

Ø26
Ø20
50
R30
R17
64.2
R20
50
25.8
R43
R40
R30

SECTION A-A

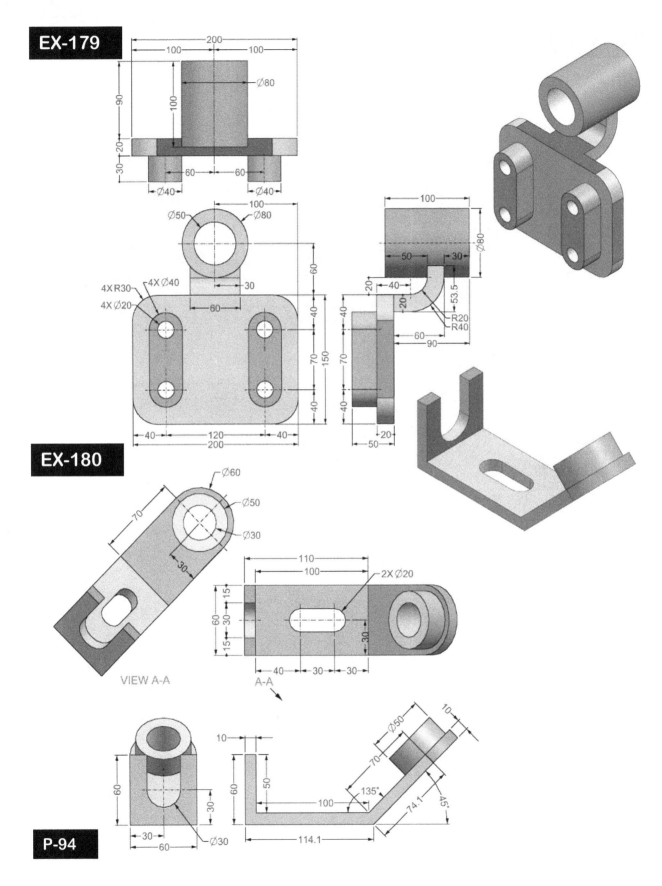

EX-179

200
100
100
Ø80
90
100
20
30
60
60
Ø40
Ø40

Ø50
100
Ø80
4XR30
4XØ40
30
4XØ20
60
60
40
70
150
40
40
120
40
200

100
Ø80
50
30
20
40
20
53.5
20
R20
R40
60
90
40
70
40
20
50

EX-180

Ø60
Ø50
70
Ø30
30

110
100
2XØ20
15
60
30
30
15
40
30
30

VIEW A-A
A-A

P-94

Ø50
10
70
60
10
50
135°
100
45°
60
30
74.1
30
60
Ø30
114.1

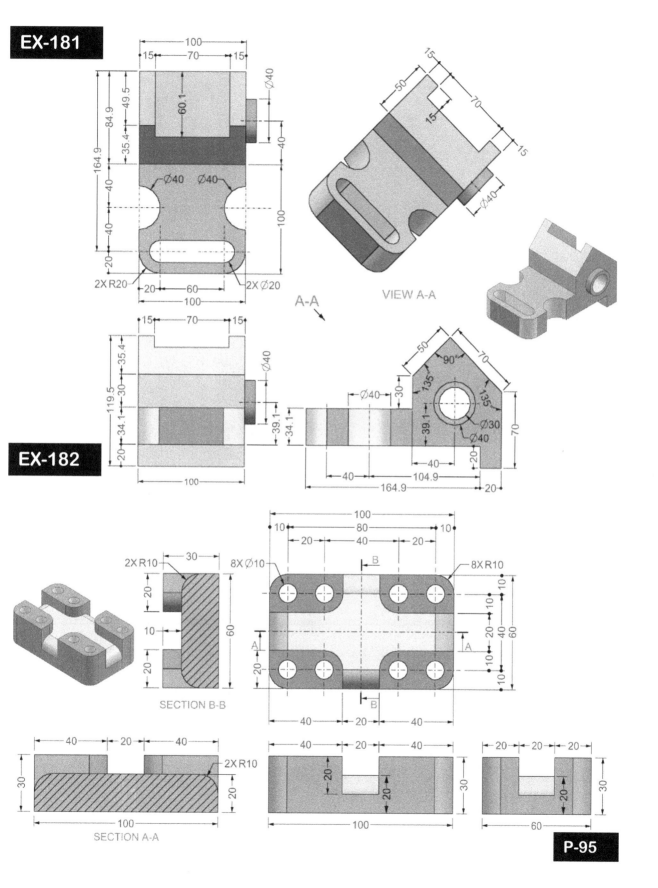

EX-181

EX-182

VIEW A-A

A-A

SECTION B-B

SECTION A-A

P-95

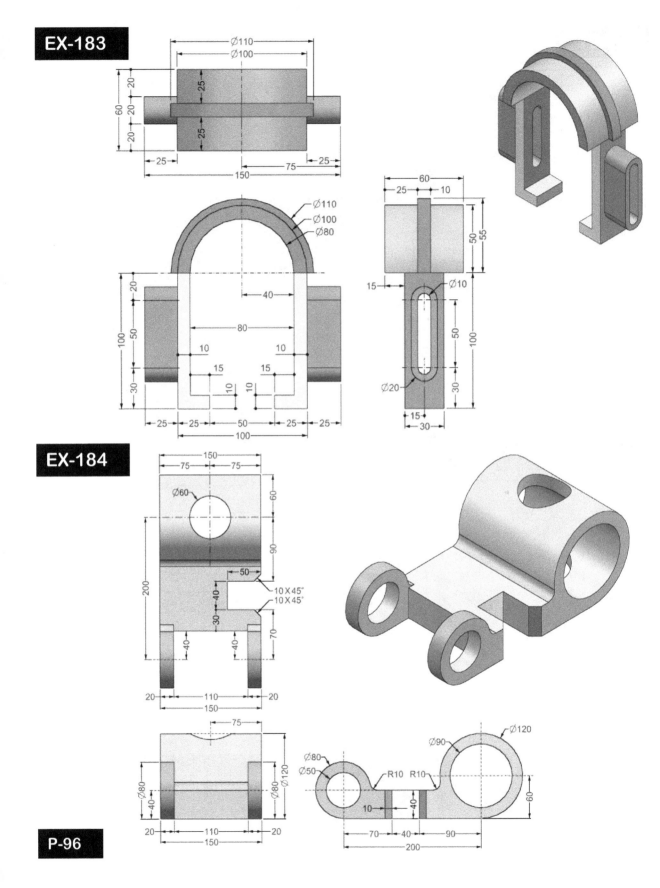

EX-183

Ø110
Ø100
20
60
20
25
20
25
25
75
25
150

Ø110
Ø100
Ø80
20
40
100
50
80
10
10
30
15
15
10
10
25
25
50
25
25
100

60
25
10
50
55
15
Ø10
50
100
Ø20
30
15
30

EX-184

150
75
75
Ø60
60
90
200
50
10 X 45°
40
30
10 X 45°
70
40
40
20
110
20
150

75
120
Ø80
Ø80
40
20
110
20
150

Ø120
Ø90
Ø80
Ø50
R10
R10
10
40
60
70
40
90
200

P-96

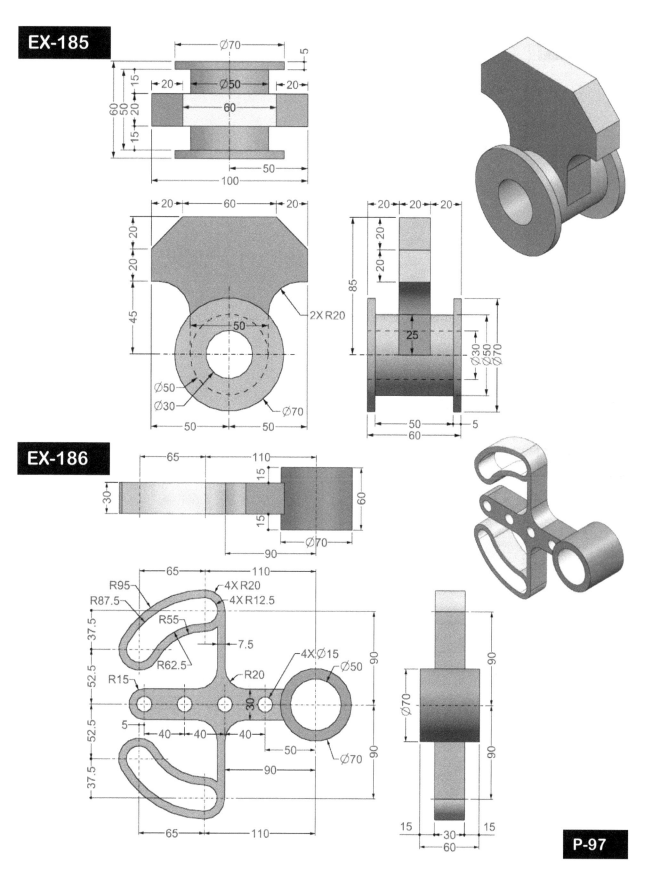

EX-185

EX-186

P-97

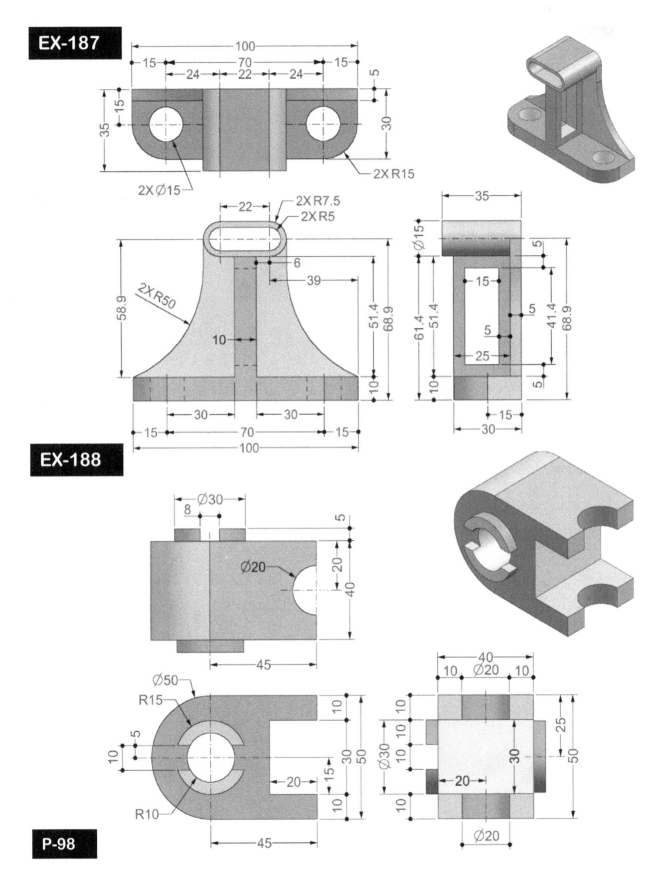

EX-187

2X Ø15
2X R15
100
15 — 70 — 15
24 — 22 — 24
35
15
30
5

2X R7.5
2X R5
22
6
39
2X R50
58.9
10
51.4
68.9
10
30 — 30
15 — 70 — 15
100

35
Ø15
5
15
61.4
51.4
68.9
5
5
41.4
25
10
5
15
30

EX-188

Ø30
8
5
20
40
Ø20
45

Ø50
R15
R10
5
10
10
30
50
15
20
10
45

40
10 Ø20 10
10
10
10
10
Ø30
30
25
50
20
10
Ø20

P-98

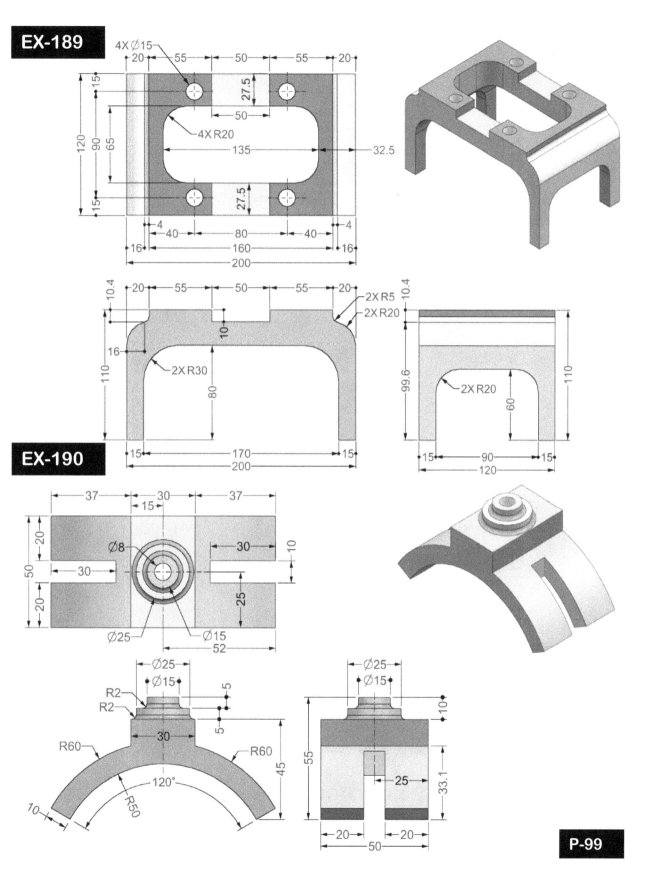

EX-189

4X Ø15
20
55
50
55
20
15
27.5
50
4X R20
90
65
135
32.5
120
15
27.5
4
40
80
40
4
16
160
16
200

10.4
20
55
50
55
20
2X R5
2X R20
10
16
2X R30
110
80
10.4
99.6
2X R20
60
110
15
170
15
15
90
15
200
120

EX-190

37
30
37
15
20
30
Ø8
30
10
50
30
25
20
Ø25
Ø15
52

Ø25
Ø15
R2
5
R2
R60
30
R60
5
R60
R60
120°
45
10
R50
Ø25
Ø15
10
55
25
33.1
20
20
50

P-99

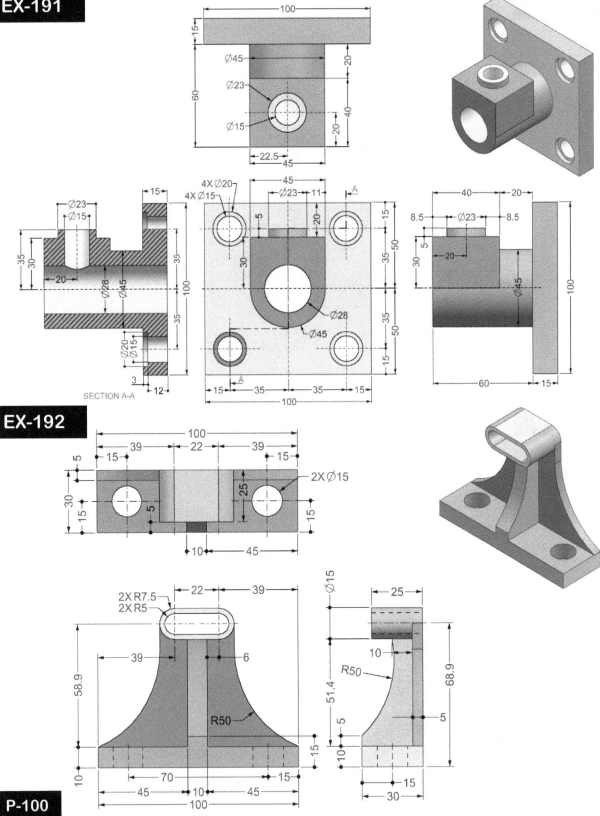

EX-191

EX-192

P-100

EX-193

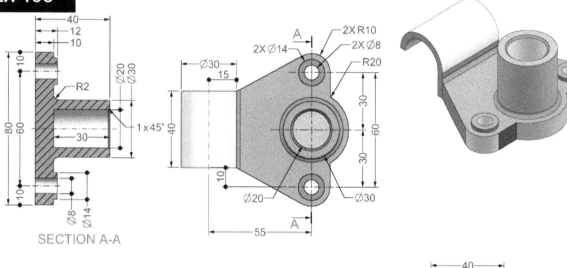

SECTION A-A

2X R10
2X Ø14
2X Ø8
R20
Ø30
15
40
30
60
30
10
Ø20
Ø30
55

40
12
10
Ø10
R2
Ø20
Ø30
80
60
30
1 x 45°
Ø10
Ø8
Ø14

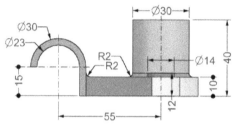

Ø30
Ø23
R2
R2
Ø30
Ø14
15
40
10
12
55

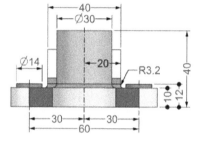

40
Ø30
Ø14
20
R3.2
10
12
40
30
30
60

EX-194

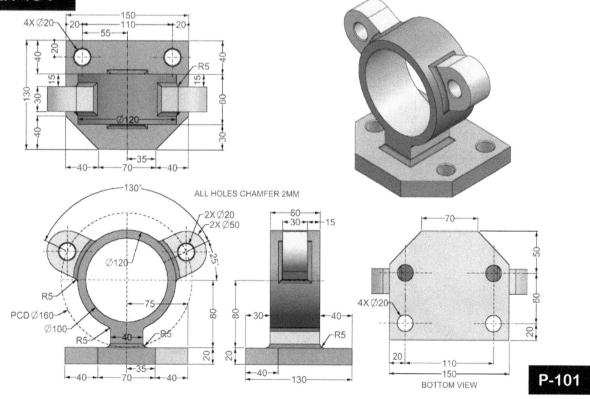

4X Ø20
150
20
110
20
55
20
40
40
15
R5
130
15
30
60
Ø120
40
30
40
70
40
35

ALL HOLES CHAMFER 2MM

130°
2X Ø20
2X Ø50
Ø120
25
R5
75
80
PCD Ø160
Ø100
R5
40
R5
20
40
70
40
35

60
30
15
80
30
40
R5
20
40
130

70
50
60
4X Ø20
20
20
110
20
150

BOTTOM VIEW

P-101

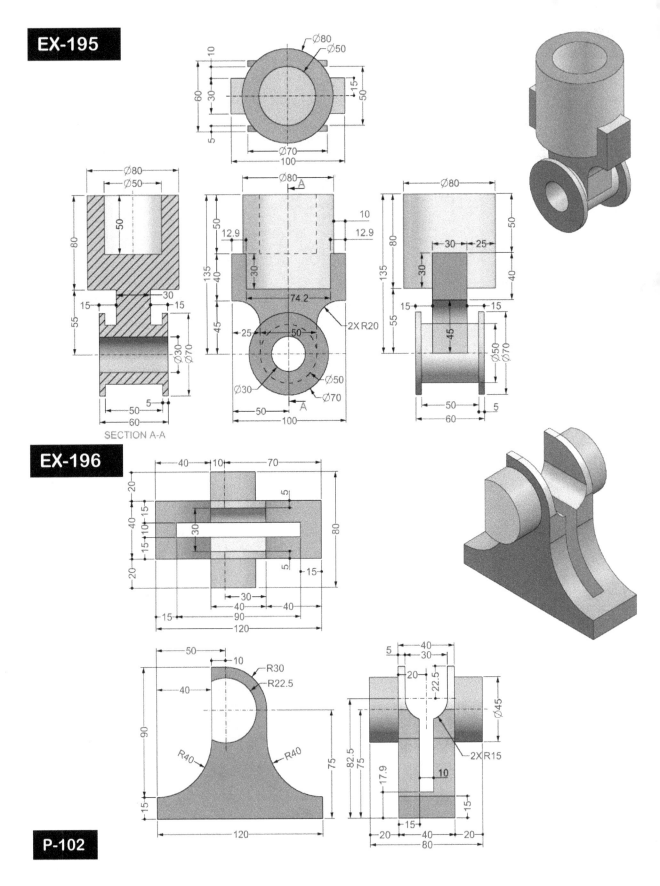

EX-195

Ø80
Ø50
10
60
30
15
50
5
Ø70
100

Ø80
Ø50
80
50
50
15
55
30
Ø30
Ø70
5
50
60
SECTION A-A

Ø80
A
50
10
135
12.9
12.9
40
30
74.2
45
25
50
2X R20
Ø30
Ø50
50
Ø70
100
A

Ø80
80
50
135
30
25
30
40
15
15
45
55
Ø50
Ø70
50
5
60

EX-196

40
10
70
20
5
40
15
15-10
30
80
15-15
20
5
15
30
40
40
15
90
120

P-102

50
10
R30
R22.5
40
90
R40
R40
75
15
120

40
5
30
20
22.5
Ø45
82.5
75
17.9
10
2X R15
15
20
40
20
80

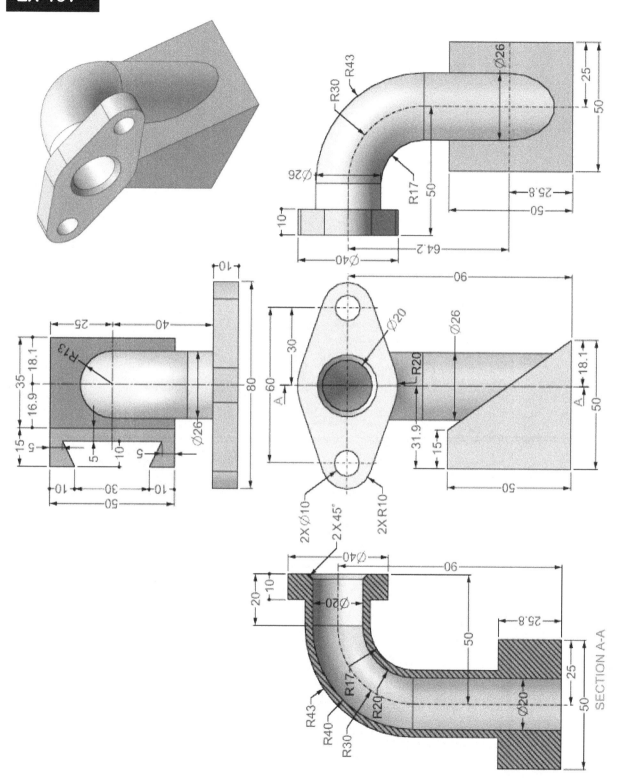

SECTION A-A

6X Ø15 THRU
ON PCD 90

Ø120

Ø50

Ø40

PCD Ø90

A

A

Ø120

Ø50

Ø40

15

10

Ø15

120

30

SECTION A-A

B-B

5

10

Ø20

Ø30

PCD 54

60°

60°

80

Ø10

VIEW B-B

Ø20

8X Ø10 THRU
ON PCD 54

Ø30

Ø70

PCD Ø54

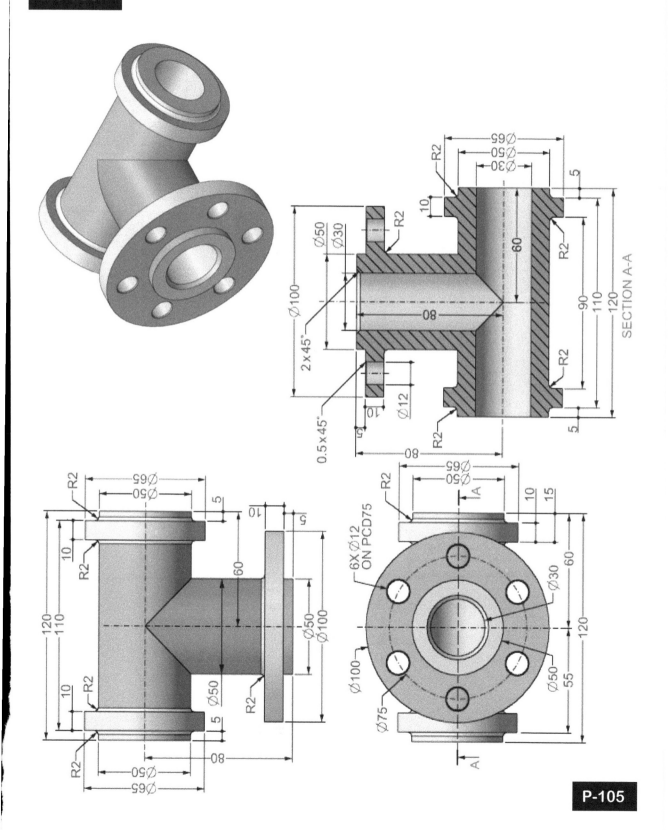

EX-199

SECTION A-A

P-105

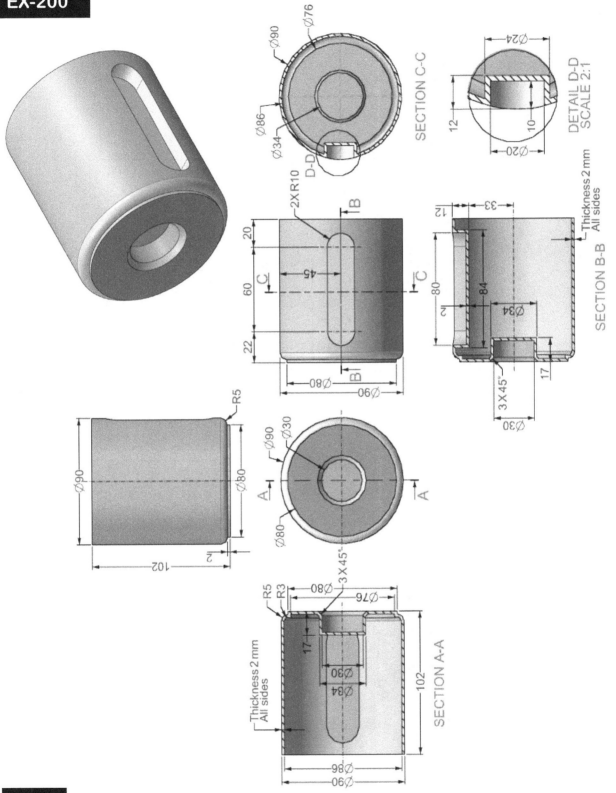

SECTION C-C

DETAIL D-D
SCALE 2:1

Ø24
Ø20
12
10

Ø90
Ø76
Ø86
Ø34
D-D

2×R10
20
60
22
Ø80
Ø90
45
B
C

SECTION B-B

Thickness 2 mm
All sides
33
12
80
84
Ø34
12
3×45°
17
Ø30

R5
Ø90
Ø80
102
2

Ø90
Ø30
Ø80
A

SECTION A-A

Thickness 2 mm
All sides
R5
R3
3×45°
Ø80
Ø76
17
Ø30
Ø84
102
Ø86
Ø90

Other useful books by CADIN360

1. 150 CAD Exercises

2. AutoCAD Exercises

3. CAD Exercises

4. 50+ SolidWorks Exercises

5. SolidWorks 200 Exercises

6. Autodesk Inventor Exercises

7. Catia Exercises

8. Siemens NX Exercises